The Farm Story: A South Dakota Memoir
© 2011 Christine Leslie Johnson

Text inside by:
Helen Ruth Ackley Johnson, 1918-2004
Jorjet Harper
Christine Leslie Johnson

Poems by Evelyn Ackley Christensen are reprinted from the book SHUTTLE SONG, available from iUniverse, 2021 Pine Lake Road, Suite 100, Lincoln, NE 68512. Copyright 2007, David E. Christensen. Reprinted with permission of the Copyright owner.

Photos by Helen Ruth Ackley Johnson, except where indicated as family photos

Book design by Kirk Williamson

On the cover: Helen Ruth Ackley Johnson, 1918-2004
Photo by Edwin E. Johnson

This book is available in both black-and-white and color editions
Price: Black-and-white edition $12.99, color edition $27
ISBN-13:978-1466490796
ISBN-10: 1466490799

Reprints of photographs are available from the publisher
Published by: Christine Leslie Johnson

Contact information:
Christine Leslie Johnson
thefarmstory.helenjohnson@gmail.com

The Farm Story
A South Dakota Memoir

by Helen Ruth Ackley Johnson

With an introduction by Jorjet Harper
and an afterword by Christine Leslie Johnson

Helen Ruth Ackley Johnson, 1918-2004.
The Ackley farm was located in the NW quarter of Section 5 Township 112 (Hartland) Range
55W Kingsbury County, South Dakota.

Dedication by Christine Leslie Johnson

Dedicated with love and gratitude to my parents,
Helen Ruth Ackley Johnson
and
Edwin Elliott Johnson

Springtime

Spring does not come to the prairie
    with a glow of soft green fire and the odor
    of bursting buds wafted on soft breezes.
It comes with rushing damp wind
    that threshes wildly the bare brittle branches
    and sends the white clouds scudding across
    an electric blue sky.—
Spring brings to plainsmen the sharp, sweet
    odor of damp brown earth.

Something in prairie spring stirs me,
    not to wanderlust.—
    not to tender thought of sweet romance,
But stirs the peasant in me to a longing.—
    to till the soil with my hands.—
    to hoe and hoe with sun hot on my back,
And finally, aching-tired, to plod homeward
    in the sunset's flaming glory.

— 1942, Evelyn Ackley Christensen (1923-2006)

Acknowledgments

Special thanks for the talents and skills of many people who helped make this book possible:

— Tracy Baim, for her generous role as publishing consultant and visionary
— Jorjet Harper, for her talented writing, researching, and editing skills
— Nancy Taylor Poore, who has contributed invaluable help throughout this project
— Kirk Williamson, for book design
— Jeanne Baker, for editing and publishing consultation
— Joyce Bolinger, for editing the "Afterword"
— Stephanie Sauder, for her help with farm updates
— Dorothy Sauder, for permission to use pictures of her
— David E. Christensen and the Christensen family, for permission to use Evelyn Ackley Christensen's poems

Table of Contents

	Introduction by Jorjet Harper	11
1	Tracing the Foundations of a Farm	17
2	Growing Family on a Growing Farm	21
3	The Old Style Farm Life	27
4	The Little Things That Matter	31
5	Visiting and Visitors	37
6	Times of Plenty	41
	Photo Section	47
7	Prairie Pastures and Pens	75
8	Household and Garden	81
9	The Rolling of the Year	87
10	Everyone Pitches In	94
11	Stormy Weather	99
12	As Time Goes By	106
	Afterword by Christine Leslie Johnson	110

Introduction

At the opening of the 20th century, the US population was around 76 million people, and more than 40% of US workers were engaged in agriculture. Forty percent! There are four times as many people in the country now than there were in 1900, and like our ancestors, we still appreciate eating every day. At the same time farm production has soared, the number of people working in agriculture has shrunk by a factor of twenty. Far fewer Americans are engaged in farming today than were a hundred years ago.

Yet the amount of land being farmed now is just about the same square acreage as it was in 1900, despite the encroachments of suburbia into rural areas by an ever-increasing populace. Over the century, while the total number of farms fell drastically (by 63%), the size of the average farm increased by a roughly equivalent amount (67%). In other words, farmland is not disappearing in the US, but farmers are.

As a lifelong city dweller, I have no real sense of what it would be like to live and work on an actual farm at any time during the 20th century. My notion of farmers was formed from characters on television, in films, and in books. Classic westerns. The Grapes of Wrath. Lassie. The musical Oklahoma. In these productions, images of The Farmer spanned the spectrum from the gullible country bumpkin to the sly, land-greedy schemer to the heroic, noble individualist plying the soil by the sweat of his brow while philosophizing on life. Possibly the only living, breathing farmer I've ever even talked with is a tall, grey-haired man in overalls who sells his organic vegetables from a covered folding table during summer market days in downtown Chicago.

I have seen what look like very picturesque, neat, and presumably successful farms from the highway between Chicago and Madison. And somewhere in the vast flatness between Chicago and St. Louis, I've had to roll up my car window while we passed through "pig farm country" breezes that wafted across the I-57. That's about it. So for me, as for most other urbanites, "farm" is little more than a concept, an abstraction. A barn and a silo at some distance from the road.

We do get complex and often alarming reports in the news about the modern "agribusiness". But these too have a distant, sometimes even science-fictiony aspect: genetically modified plants and seeds, the use of growth hormones in dairy cows and chickens, the corporate patenting of genes and breeding techniques, and so on. Often it's difficult to even assess which of these developments are good and which are bad. A bit closer to home are the reports about the growth of organic farming and the local produce movement, and we may pay more attention to these trends since we can see them unfold at our supermarkets and local groceries.

Today, 1.3% of all US farms account for 42% of the value of US farm production. It's hardly surprising that agriculture, once so central in American experience, has been radically altered during a century when changes in many other industries have transformed our overall economic realities so dramatically. But whatever we may think about the automotive industry or steel production, there is still something more primal about agriculture—and more intimate. Unlike cars and steel girders, agriculture involves products that we put in our bodies, that we cannot live without, that we shop for on a daily basis.

Intensive farming methods have increased farm yields per acre enormously, and US agricultural exports today are many times greater than they were in 1918, the year Helen Ackley was born on a small farm in South Dakota. Helen grew up in a farm family in the decades between the two World Wars. As an adult, witnessing the huge changes taking place during her own generation, she realized that the way of life she had been brought up into was being so transformed by technology and other factors that it was changed forever, and she took photos and wrote about her experiences to describe what family farm life was like, before it disappeared.

When I read the manuscript of Helen's account, and saw the photos she took of this land she knew so well, it resonated for me in a way the history books and fiction I have read about those times had not—perhaps precisely because it is a personal memoir of one woman's life growing up on a farm, so I could see it in a context stripped of statistics and hot button topics and idealized entertainment-industry portraits. Helen describes in detail the day-to-day activities of a true farm family—her own. She grew up among hardworking, earnest people whose entire lives were, in one way or another, tied to the land, and she tells us about their farming and household tasks and community clearly and informationally, without the saccharin and bathetic fictions of farm life we see so often on television and in films. Life and land are unified for this family in a way hardly imaginable to modern city dwellers like me.

Helen's narrative and photos present real people who managed to make a living from the land in the days before electricity, refrigeration, and running water. She explains how the introduction of each new 20th century innovation in farming and in communication began to affect their way of life, ultimately becoming more specialized, mechanized, and standardized.

1935 was a pivotal year in the history of US agriculture, because that was the year the number of farms in the US reached nearly 7 million, the peak from which they have been declining ever since. Farm products made up almost 8% of the US economy at that time. Today there are under 2 million farms, and while the market value of farm products is greater than ever, in relation to the overall US economy that value has shrunk tenfold. Helen turned 17 in the spring of that highest-farm year of 1935, and it was a pivotal year for her as well: that fall her grandfather died—the man who, with his wife and children, had founded the Ackley farm that sustained four generations of their family.

Helen was deeply interested in documenting her family and its origins. There were earlier "editions" of The Farm Story that Helen handed out to her relatives from time to time as she did research and wrote, but in 1990 she finished the definitive version, the culmination of her Farm Story project that you are about to read in the pages that follow. When Helen began writing it, she felt it was important to distinguish between the facts she knew (genealogy, deeds, land purchases and so on) and personal memories and anecdotes. She highlighted this difference by typing the factual, reportorial paragraphs in a Roman font, and her more personal memories in a script font. Once she got further into the story, however, she dispensed with this distinction. "From here on, my story is all about the things I remember; and I will not set apart my first person memories in different type," she wrote. Ever practical, she added that also "The 'Courier' is easier to read." (In this new edition, the font changes have been eliminated altogether.) I like to think she made this decision to consolidate her narrative into one font as she became more confident of her voice as a writer.

Included in that 1990 manuscript was a foreword in the form of a letter to her relatives, dated September of that year, in which Helen touched upon her goals and took ownership of her writing process: "Dear Family," she wrote, "When I started this—quite a few years ago—I intended to make it my sisters' and my story; but I found I couldn't write from three people's perspective. Therefore, these are my memories and my words." She admitted to the reader that the "old offset machine leaves much to be desired when it comes to printing, and some of the pages are smudged—but that is what we had to use. Edwin [her husband] did his best with an old machine and a second-hand copier."

Helen credited her younger sister Dorothy with encouraging her "to finish this story, and for having most of the pictures printed. We decided to use prints," she explained, "because offset copies of these old farm pictures would not have been clear. The prints were mostly those taken by Dad and Mother in the early years of their marriage." Helen signed this letter with love.

The photo prints Helen had gathered together for that 1990 manuscript were laid out in a separate section, with captions. In addition to the photos taken by her parents, there were images that Helen took herself during the war years with the camera Edwin had left in her keeping while he was overseas. Film was difficult to get during World War II; the only type commercially available to Helen was Kodacolor slide film, and using this film, Helen became a skilled, sensitive photographer, amassing a large collection of vintage photos. These slide images captured some of the farm machinery in action, the people, the landscapes, and the beauty of her surroundings that became an integral part of her project for The Farm Story.

Helen also embedded illustrations in her text. These came from a 1908 Sears & Roebuck catalog (and are not reprinted here). One of her goals was to explain how they did everything on the farm, so in order to illustrate an appliance or a machine that she had not taken a photo of, she went through the catalog, clipped out the relevant pictures, and pasted them close to where they were mentioned. "They are not exactly like the ones we had," she commented, but they were "typical" of the type of machines she saw every day on the farm.

Near her description of pig butchering, for instance, she placed a picture of a large family-size meat chopper, selling for $2.45, and a stuffer and presser that could be used as a sausage stuffer, a lard press, and even a wine press, priced at $4.05. By her description of the farm kitchen's large Monarch cast iron cook stove, she placed a steel kitchen range that cost $11.98. She also provided clip art of a cream separator (a model that looked kind of like a Dalek on skis with a spout and handcrank), a butter churn, two types of clothes wringers, a purifying water pump, a manure spreader, and all sorts of harnesses, carriages for horses, plows, posthole diggers, and combines. It had never occurred to me that a farmer could purchase an entire windmill, but Sears & Roebuck offered them, starting at $35.45.

Another thing I had never heard of before reading The Farm Story was the Chautauqua movement. Apparently in an age before television, the Chautaqua was a seasonal staple in rural entertainment. Thousands of communities across America, and many millions of people, participated in them in the first three decades of the 1900s. These tent shows featured educational talks, musical performances, pep rallies delivered by motivational speakers of the day, entertainers presenting stories and morality tales, and lecturers on popular religious topics. Helen remembered "sitting on benches or wooden chairs under a large tent, with grass underfoot, watching a magician," and "choral programs with a good male chorus, plays ... travel lectures and instrumental music." She tells us how she and her cousins trapped gophers to earn the $2 each they needed for a summer season ticket. "The Chautauqua was the high point of the summer for the few years it set up tent in Bryant, about 1930, give or take a couple of years," she recalled.

Like so much in The Farm Story, this left me wishing Helen had told us even more about the activities of rural and small-town South Dakota in those days, and about the ideas and opinions of the day. Helen has little to say about local politics, tells us nothing about race relations in South Dakota, mentions the Depression and World War II only as these events impact her farm and her family, and speaks about religion solely in the context of her own family's church experiences. While I would have liked to know more of Helen's thoughts on any of these topics, there's a certain honesty in the way she chooses her words. She keeps her tone, as much as possible, factual, reporting on the changing farm work as the seasons change, and surviving crises like dust storms and fires. She knows the topography of the subjects she intends to tell us about, and while she warms to including more personal musings as she goes along, overall she keeps her eye on the plow.

She also doesn't say very much about interpersonal relationships between the people in the family, and this is another aspect of her story I would have liked to learn more about. I get the impression that, in general, these were not people who dwelled on or talked about their feelings. Her sparse, stick-to-the-facts style is, in itself, a demonstration of 20th century Midwestern thinking, and may give us some hints about how these people were able to tough it out together in the isolation of the sweeping prairie panorama. Privacy in one's emotions, whether joy or grief, seems to have been paramount.

Helen's writing style sometimes approaches the poetic while her subject remains ever-rooted in the practical. "There were no more horses in the barn; tractors did the work, and they got bigger and bigger. Harvesting probably changed the most—combines went through the fields, cutting and threshing the ripe grain and emptying it into tractor-pulled wagons or trucks to be hauled to the elevator or stored in bins. Often the grain was cut, wind-rowed, and allowed to dry for a few days before being picked up and threshed by the combine." Her descriptions of her final visit to the farm, seeing what was left of it, are spare and dignified yet poignant.

In her foreword to the 1990 edition, she said, "I invite others to write their own memories and add them. I have enjoyed sharing mine." I found this very touching, since she meant it for her family's chronicles, but it applies to everyone generally. We need more of such accounts, from people who are not professional writers but who can tell us vividly and clearly about their occupations and the events of their lives. They need to be shared and heard and encouraged. Every day, information about how "ordinary" objects used to work, "ordinary" tasks used to be accomplished, "ordinary" opinions used to be expressed, and "ordinary" new ideas and innovations were once created becomes lost to us and lost to the future.

Except for the spotlights on the wealthy and famous, so little of human experience and activity has survived down through the centuries told by the people who lived it. It's obvious why this has happened, but in our age of almost universal literacy—and the technology of keyboards and cameras and recorders and new modes of publication—personal histories like Helen's have a much better chance of surviving the filter of history. This grassroots history stands as a counterweight to the sensationalist celebrity stories that flood our media. If "ordinary people" don't tell us what their lives mean to them, and what life was like around them, then how are we to know?

In essence, The Farm Story answers that question. It is an act of faith: a long, thoughtful, loving letter from Helen, reaching out to her future family and descendants, explaining to them a way of life that she realized they would never know if she didn't tell them. Appreciating what she has to say makes each new reader a part of her extended family, too. She touches on the bold outlines of American History as she knew them, but mostly she stands firmly at eye level, speaking through her words and her camera lens, giving us a window into a way of life that has, indeed, now vanished from the landscape of American experience.

— Jorjet Harper, Editor

1

Tracing the Foundations of a Farm

For almost seventy years, a farmhouse on the northwest quarter of a square mile of South Dakota prairie sheltered four generations of the family of Ed and Ida Ackley. Ed and Ida came from Illinois and bought the farm in 1902. Ten members of four generations of Ackley descendants lived for at least some time on the farm, and more than seventy people can trace their ancestry to this couple—my grandparents.

No family needs this house and farmyard for a home any more. All of its children have scattered. Farms are larger now, and it requires at least three or four times as much land to support a family in these days of large tractors. As I write this in 1990, many sites where a farmyard used to be are now fields of grain or corn.

When we go back to South Dakota in the summer, I always like to pay a visit to that farm where I was born and grew up, even though only a few landmarks remain that look like home.

The ash trees I transplanted from the Tree Claim to my flower bed remain, as does the lilac hedge that Mother and I planted with sprouts from the hedge in back of the garden of my Ackley grandparents' home in Bryant, South Dakota.

Along the south fence, asparagus and rhubarb, probably as old as the farm, or at the latest planted by my grandmother, struggle to compete with the tall grass of the hayfield that now occupies the yard.

The big red barn—the horse barn—is leaning but it still stands. All the other buildings are moved or destroyed. The farmhouse has been torn down, and its lumber used elsewhere. A few of its old square nails have been saved as souvenirs.

One can feel sadness at the passing of an era without wishing to return to it or perpetuate it. Nostalgia has a place in all of our lives, however. It may bring pleasure to some of the grandchildren and great-grandchildren who visited the farm to recall what life there was like.

Edward Ackley, called Ed by his friends, was born in Chilicothe, Peoria County, Illinois on 12 August 1854, the second son of John and Jane (Nixon) Ackley.

John, Edward's father, had been a teamster. Chilicothe was situated along the Illinois River, north of Peoria, and produce was brought to Chilicothe for shipment downriver by boat, or north to Chicago by team-and-wagon. Farmers drove their hogs to an area called Camp Grove, near the river, where for a few years they held cooperative hog killing and processing. The pork would be salted and packed into barrels for shipment. One of the first industries in Chilicothe was a flour mill, which ground the grain raised nearby and gave farmers a market for their produce.

Edward moved with his parents and older brother Henry to a farm in Stark County, Illinois in 1860. There he grew up, finished school, and then went to a Normal School in Valparaiso, Indiana to prepare himself to teach. He had a great love and respect for learning, and a fine mind. Afflicted with asthma since childhood, he was probably more comfortable in the classroom than in the fields.

Edward taught in the rural schools of Stark and nearby Fulton Counties for some years, and eventually purchased a farm of 80 acres near the town of Wyoming, Illinois. In Fulton County, Edward met tiny Mary Ida Maxwell (called Ida all of her life), another school teacher, and soon began courting her.

Ida was the youngest of three children of Jaccob and Lydia (Loper) Maxwell. Her father Jaccob had been killed in the Civil War when she was five years old. Ed and Ida were married on 21 March 1883, in the home of her mother and stepfather, Isaac Ellis, in Fulton County. He was 29 years old and she 24.

The young couple lived on their farm (in Penn Township—N half of NW half of Sec. 22, Twp 13, R7E, 4th M). Some years they hired a man to do the farm work while Ed taught school. Three sons were born to them: Leslie Edward on 24 April 1886, Carroll Maxwell (called Carl) on 23 July 1887, and John Bliss (called Bliss) on 1 June 1898. Leslie and Carl completed grade school and began high school in the town of Wyoming.

Edward's asthma continued to give him trouble, and he began to think about moving to a drier climate, which was one of the few remedies doctors could suggest at that time. He visited Denver, one recommended area, but decided instead to move to South Dakota. Some friends and neighbors from Illinois had already moved there, and reported good rich soil.

With the decision made, Ed and Ida sold their 80-acre farm in Penn Township for $6000 to Robert Adams, with possession to be given 1 March 1901. In July of that year they bought the quarter section in South Dakota, paying $4000 for a farm twice the size of the one they were leaving. But apparently they did not move to their new home until the spring of 1902; in those days, March First was the usual agreed-upon moving time for farm families.

When the family moved from the farm near Wyoming, Illinois to Kingsbury County, South Dakota, Ida Ackley rode in the comfort of a passenger train with her youngest son Bliss, who was nearly 4 years old. Edward, with sons Leslie, 15, and Carl, 14, rode in the caboose of the freight train when they were not attending to the livestock in the "immigrant" car that was part of the train. They probably went by a branch line of the railroad to Chicago and from there west to Sioux Falls where the freight car was joined to a northbound freight to Bryant, South Dakota. Whether they realized it or not, they rode through a corner of their new home farm.

Today, the South Dakota farmland where the Ackley family arrived in 1902 has been cultivated for over 100 years, yet it is still very new compared to the farms of Europe or even to those in the eastern states. Before 1883, the area was prairie grassland, part of the Dakota Territory. In October of 1883, much of what had been Sioux Indian land was opened to white settlement. Those who recognized the value of the soil and wanted their own land, or better land, were quick to come and take advantage of their rights under the Homestead Act of 1863.

In the first month of new settlement, October 1883, James P. Barker and his wife Eliza filed a homestead claim to this quarter section of prairie at the District Land Office in Watertown. Probably the house and oldest barn were built that first year, because James Barker borrowed money, mortgaging the land.

On 9 September 1886, three years after settling on the farm, James Barker sold "a strip of land extending across from east side to north side, 100 feet wide" to the Dakota and Great Southern Railway for $1.00. Access to a railroad was a necessity in order to send crops to market and to buy machinery and all the other things he couldn't raise.

James and Eliza lived on their claim for the required five years, improved it as the law required, and received the patent from the United States on 10 August 1888. The Barkers mortgaged the land, and paid off the mortgage, several times before they finally sold it to George T. Cole on 2 January 1897, for $1200, except for a mortgage of $750 and back taxes for 1895 and 1896. By that time, the Milwaukee Railroad had acquired the right-of-way of the Dakota and Great Southern.

The farm changed hands again a year later when the Coles sold it to E.O. Schjeldahl for $1700, and again on 28 March 1899, when it was sold to George W. Hart, this time for $2800. George and Myrtle Hart had owned the farm for two years when they sold it on 1 July 1901 to Edward E. Ackley for $4000.

The Ackley family moved into a white-painted frame house of six rooms, with a small kitchen and a trap door in the dining room floor to the cellar underneath. Upstairs were two bedrooms. There were the usual farm buildings: a horse and cow barn, hog barn, chicken house, coal shed, and privy. It is possible that the granary and the tool shed that stood beside the windmill were also built before 1902; the number of structures on the property Edward Ackley bought was not listed in the deed, and no one is living now who remembers.

A row of ash trees lined the driveway north of the house and only slightly broke the force of the winter northwest winds. There was a fenced garden between the house and the graded dirt road which marked the west side of Section 5. Beside the door was a cistern that held the runoff water from the house roof—this was the water supply for family use. At this time there was no pump, and all water was lifted from the cistern in a bucket.

A deep artesian well provided water for the livestock. This well did have a pump, with a windmill to power it. Although the well tapped the artesian aquifer, it was not in an area where there was enough pressure to force the water to the surface. The farm's first well had been dug in a ravine, south and a little east of the buildings, and it was a shallow well, curbed with wood. No records remain to tell when the first deep well was drilled beside the barn, but it served for many years until the pipe curbing deteriorated and a new well had to be drilled. I think the new well must have been drilled in the late 1940s, because I was no longer at home when it was done.

Water from the well by the barn was very cold, but it was also very hard, and we didn't drink it unless we were doing chores at the barn and were hot and thirsty. Grandma said this well water was so hard "that you couldn't boil beans in it," meaning they would never get tender. (I used to think that was just a figure of speech until I read in later years that it was true, due to the high mineral content.) We used to have an old bucket nailed to the wooden water tank directly under the end of the pipe, and there we cooled tea, or sometimes soft drinks, or the root beer that Dad made.

The farm was probably average in its appearance and operation during the earliest years of the 20th century. Edward and his sons were hardworking men and good farmers, but not innovative. Leslie, especially, was good at fixing machinery, and kept fences in good repair. The animals were well cared for, especially the horses, for their health was vital to the farm. They had no riding horses. They weren't interested in riding, and felt no need for a showy buggy horse, although the farm boasted two single buggies, and there were runners for a small cutter sleigh hanging in the tool shed.

The men made no attempt to beautify the yard or to have a special lawn around the house.

The most convenient arrangement for mowing the grass a couple of times during the summer was the order of things, and any more trees or shrubs, or even fences, would have made it harder to mow the yard with the hay mower. Ida had a flower garden next to the coal shed, where she could easily see it from the south window of the dining room.

The town of Erwin was four-and-a-half miles to the southeast. Edward was drawn to the Erwin community because it was the place where he voted. He invested in the Erwin Farmers Elevator there, owned stock in it, and was elected secretary/treasurer. He and Ida joined the Woodmen and Royal Neighbors in that community and were part of its social life. They were really part of both the Erwin and Bryant communities, and had friends in both places, but over the years they were drawn more in the direction of Bryant. It was closer—three-and-a-half miles. Their mail came from Bryant, and Ida and Leslie, at least, attended the Baptist Church there. Bryant had more stores, and they usually went there on Saturdays to "trade" eggs and cream for the groceries they needed. Leslie and Carl both went to high school in Bryant and made friends there.

As he had hoped, Edward's health was improved the first years after he moved to South Dakota, and he was able to work in the fields. Leslie and Carl both worked on the farm, finished high school, and then went away for at least another year of education. Leslie went to business college in Des Moines, Iowa, and Carl to a school in Mandan, North Dakota. Bliss finished grade school at the one-room school three-quarters-of-a-mile south of the farm and then went to Brookings Ag School for his high school years.

2

A Growing Family on a Growing Farm

In 1908, six years after Edward Ackley and his sons began farming the northwest quarter of Section 5, the southeast quarter came up for sale, and they decided to buy it.

This was a tree claim, and had been planted with a half-mile-long grove of ash trees, ten or 12 rows wide, and "proved up" in this way. (In the summer of 1977, when my sister Evelyn and I went to South Dakota for the final reunion of our school at Erwin before it closed, Mark Atwood of De Smet told me that he remembered helping his father plant that grove of trees, as a very young boy.)

There were no farm buildings on the new quarter, and it was divided by the railroad right-of-way, which cut through it from south to north.

Now the farm was almost doubled in size. The northwest or home quarter was actually 20 acres larger than the usual 160 acres, because of the correction line: In order to continue uniformly square miles on the curved surface of the earth, tiers of townships of square miles did not match. There was a jog in the north-south roads all along this line.

In these years when the farm prospered, improvements were made in the buildings—a big new red barn with a large haymow, for horses only; a smoke house to cure hams and bacon and a privy to match; a new hog barn.

Field work was done with teams of two to six horses, and there were always twelve to fourteen horses in the barn. There was machinery for two teams: two cultivators, two plows, two grain binders, two hayracks, two triple-box wagons. One grain drill was enough, however, and one mower, one rake, one potato planter and one digger. Some of the small machines are now collectors' items—a fanning mill (to clean seed grain), a potato cutter (to cut potatoes into chunks for planting), a hand corn sheller, a rope maker, a set of pipe threaders.

The Ackley family found its place in the community, and the sons grew up. Leslie and Carl worked with their father on the farm, and each made a decision—Leslie to stay on the farm, and Carl to strike out on his own.

Edward, as time went on, was more troubled with asthma. Leslie had taken over most of the operation of the farm with Bliss, who came back to live at home after finishing Ag School in Brookings.

In July of 1912, Leslie, at age 25, married Sarah Owens. She came to the farm to live, but died of flu in September of that same year. Four years after Sarah died, Leslie married Verna Griffith, on 18 October 1916. He had met her and her family at the Baptist Church in Bryant, and had become good friends with her father, C.D. Griffith.

I and my sisters Evelyn and Dorothy—the children of Leslie and Verna—were all born on the farm and grew up there. We girls were aware of Dad's first wife, and Dad's trunk in the attic room held a few things which had been Sarah's. I remember a stretchy gold bracelet which I was allowed to wear, and a boxed manicure set of scissors, nail file, and buffer, all with white handles.

When I was in grade school, a new family with two children moved into the district. The girl in my grade told me that her parents had known my Dad before his first marriage, and insisted that I was Sarah's daughter! I finally found the courage to ask my Mother about it, and she assured me that I was not Sarah's daughter, but hers.

When Uncle Carl first left the farm, he tried his hand at editing a newspaper in Lake Norden, but the paper was not a success, and he went to North Dakota to teach school. There he met Nellie Toepke, who was teaching in Glen Ullin, and in a few months they were married in Nellie's home near Judson. The date was 13 December 1913. Carl took his bride by train to Bryant during the Christmas holiday to meet his family.

Many years later, Nellie recalled an incident from that first train ride to Bryant that she told to her oldest daughter, Doris. While on the train, she said, Carl lost his billfold, and his quick temper caused a furor. He was sure someone had stolen it—but it was soon found between the seats!

In the spring after his marriage, Carl and a friend, LeRoy Keeney, bought a farm near Mentor, Minnesota, and went there to put in a crop while Nellie and Keeney's wife Elsie finished teaching the school term before joining them. The next year they sold the farm and went back to Judson to teach school again. Carl and Nellie continued to live in Judson until 1918, when Carl got a job with the Northern Pacific Railroad. From then on, until his death in 1939, the family lived in several different towns in Montana and North Dakota. Ten children—five boys and five girls—were born to them, and all grew to maturity. Carl taught school for 11 years and worked for the railroad for 21 years before his death.

Leslie and Carl's younger brother, my Uncle Bliss, attended the one-room school that was located on a triangle of virgin prairie on the corner of a section about three-quarters-of-a-mile south of the farm, and then he went to the Ag School. He never married, and lived the rest of his life on the farm.

Along about 1918, another 80 acres were added to the farm when Leslie bought the south half of the northeast quarter—thus joining the two original quarters more solidly together.

Mom told me once that when Dad proposed to her, he promised to build them a house of their own, north of the old farmhouse. Instead, he bought this 80 acres, and I never learned why. Perhaps land prices were going up and he decided that they could live as they had been for a few years and build a house later. Perhaps Grandpa had already planned by then to retire to town.

While he was courting Verna Griffith, Leslie had bought a Kodak camera that took postcard size pictures. With this camera, he began to record the various events of the farm year, capturing quite a good record of farm life in South Dakota in the late Teens and early Twenties of this century. He also took photos of family gatherings, of farm animals and pets, and then, of course, photos of his new daughter.

On 6 April 1918, Leslie and Verna's first child was born—me—and so began the third generation to live on the farm. It was also the start of a time of great change in the life of the farm and its family. This change didn't happen all at once, and no one noticed it happening, but new inventions and new attitudes would transform life on farms more in a few years' time than had ever happened in a like period of time before.

One of these changes was right on the wall. The telephone line was extended south from Bryant, and in 1921, a telephone was installed on the west wall of the farm house dining room. The farm was now connected with doctors, businesses, and my maternal grandparents.

Each of the five or six families on the line could hear everyone's ring, and frequently listened if they thought the conversation might be interesting or if they didn't have anything better to do. The farm's ring was two long and one short. You had to call the operator (Central) to talk to anyone other than the people on the line. Neighbors who lived south and west of the farm for a few miles came to make calls because there were no other telephones in their areas. Quite often, someone came in the middle of the night to call a doctor. One man insisted that he couldn't hear over that contraption and always had someone else relay his messages.

With six people of three generations living in the small farm house—my grandparents, parents, Uncle Bliss, and I—more room was needed, and Edward decided to enlarge it.

One of the first needs was a larger cellar, and this was accomplished by digging under the house on the west side and tunneling under the house to the old cellar. A hole large enough to admit an earth scraper was made, and an iron scraper lowered into the old cellar. Here the digging had to be done by hand, the scraper filled and then hauled out by a team of horses hitched to it by a couple of log chains. During the digging, two or three large boulders were found. They had to be dug out and hauled up in the scraper. These boulders had been deposited in one of the glacial periods more than 10,000 years ago.

My memories of the events of life on the farm begins with this activity. I remember the straining effort of the team of horses as they dug in their hooves and pulled out the heavy scraper with its load of earth or large rock. I remember watching the excavation from the safe arms of an adult—looking down from that height on the whole operation. The rocks were hauled into the pigpen to where there were some scrubby trees, and there they stayed, making an interesting place to play when I was older.

The cellar was walled with brick, but was left with a dirt floor. A new stairway was added south of the small kitchen, and after that, the trap door in the floor of the dining room was no longer used.

Another addition to the house was a third bedroom upstairs. The roof over the dining room was raised to make room for a bedroom with windows on the south and west.

1921 was also the year that Leslie and Bliss bought the farm's first automobile, a Hudson "touring" car with a fold-down top (which was never folded down) and side curtains with isinglass windows which could be buttoned on in cold or wet weather. It had small "jump seats" folded against the back of the front seat, but these were never used unless all other seats were full.

The alleyway of the granary served as the car's garage. There was a family story about Mother learning to drive the car into the granary and learning how to use the brake, but she denied this and insisted that it was Uncle Bliss who had to open the doors on both ends of the alleyway at first. Then, if he could not stop where he was supposed to, he could drive on through and around to try again! I believed her—she was always a good driver.

Grandpa would not learn to drive the car, although he would ride in it. He preferred driving Sally, the small white horse, hitched to one of the buggies.

It was also in 1921 that the rural school districts in the township voted on a consolidation agreement, and it passed. The men of the family actively opposed this, because they were sure it would raise taxes but not necessarily raise the quality of education. They had been taught in one-room schools, going on for higher education in nearby towns, and they knew it was possible to get a good education in that way.

After the vote to consolidate had been approved, a new brick building was built in Erwin, and five dark green school buses brought in the children of the township, grades one through twelve. It was here that my sisters and I went to school when each of us was old enough to attend.

My sisters and I always felt on the fringes of both Erwin and Bryant, never quite belonging to either town's communities. Our church was in Bryant—and since our grandparents lived there, family activities off the farm were always centered in Bryant—but our school was in Erwin.

1922—the year after the school consolidation issue—would have been one of the first elections in which Mom and Grandma had the right to vote, and I wish I could remember anything that was said about their voting for the first time. They probably voted as soon as they could, and probably voted the way the men of the family did.

Grandpa had been right about the taxes going up—they doubled in 1922. Many years later, I came across his tax receipt for the first half of that year, and saw that he had scrawled across it, "Paid under protest!"

Grandpa Ackley was a methodical man, and he saved important things like tax receipts and cancelled checks. After he and Grandma moved to Bryant in 1924, these early tax receipts went into the possession of Uncle Bliss. They were put away in his trunk, not to be found again until after his death. The bundle of those receipts, recording the amount of taxes from the time Grandpa bought the farm until the time he moved to town, told a rather interesting story.

From 1903 until 1926, the taxes on the northwest quarter section increased tenfold, from $21.08 in 1903 to $207.42. The years 1917/18 saw the tax double from $47.12 to $101.50. In 1922, when the first increase for the consolidated school was levied, they went from $110.56 to $206.34. The tree claim quarter, purchased in 1907, was taxed $25.74 that year, and it rose from $89.28 in 1921 to $175.04 in 1922. By 1926 it was down to $160.70. Taxes on personal property were $5.22 in 1903 and they rose gradually, but unevenly, to a high of $37.18 in 1920. Grandpa also paid a $1 poll tax every year; Dad started paying this tax when he was 21 in 1909, and Uncle Bliss in 1919.

From 1908 to 1917 the tax bill included $1 for a dog tax. Since neither my parents nor grandparents ever mentioned any of the dogs they may have had during this time, I know nothing about them. The money was used to compensate farmers for sheep, pigs, or calves which were sometimes killed by packs of dogs running them at night.

It must have been an all-day trip to De Smet to pay taxes twice a year by horse and buggy, though I am sure they could have been paid by a check in the mail. Somehow I imagine that Grandpa chose to go to the county seat and pay his taxes in person!

Grandpa and Grandma decided to spend the winter of 1921/22 in Texas, in the hope that Grandpa's asthma would not bother him so much in a warmer climate. They went by train to Brownsville, Texas, where they rented housekeeping rooms. Grandma enjoyed the warmth, the new friends, and the relaxed atmosphere very much; I think that Grandpa was interested in seeing a new place and learning how different crops were raised in the south. They sent home grapefruit, and the first "blood" oranges we had ever seen.

Something my parents discussed that I remember clearly—it impressed me, I guess—was Grandpa's attitude toward eating lettuce. Grandpa had talked with a truck gardener in the area who was feeding the outside leaves of his market lettuce to his cow. The man said that the cow liked them, but something in the lettuce made her sleepy or dopey. After he heard that, Grandpa didn't think much of lettuce!

Shortly after my grandparents came home at Easter time, we had a late snow storm, the worst storm of the whole winter, and it blew in high snow banks between the house and the barn. Dad got out his camera and took a picture of Grandma and me standing on a snow bank that was so high it almost obscured the chicken house. Grandma was wearing her fur coat, and I had on a heavy coat, cap, scarf, leggings, and one-buckle overshoes. These overshoes had cloth uppers and rubber soles, but were not high enough to give much protection—hence, the leggings.

Part of the space under the new roof had been partitioned off from the bedroom to make a sort of attic, for storage. You could still stand up when you were just inside the attic door, but the roof sloped sharply to the floor, making an unfinished closet about 8 feet wide and 12 feet long.

This became my favorite place to be alone. The chimney from the cellar went up through the kitchen, and in the attic there was a small window on the south, near the floor, that would not open. The warmth of the chimney made it a fairly comfortable spot in which to read in the winter time, especially if it was a sunny day. I explored a lot of the books that were stored in this attic, which we called "the closet room", while I sat by that window on blankets or pillows.

We had more than 300 books of various kinds there, under the eaves in one corner. Dad and Uncle Bliss bought the novels of the day, and there were school text books saved by all the older members of the family—saved from the days when everyone bought his/her own books and none were provided free. Grandpa's grammar and mathematics books, a leather-bound history of the Civil War, the books on crops and animal husbandry that Uncle Bliss had in Ag School, Mother's beautifully hand-written notebooks on history and geography, the classics that she and Dad had read in high school—all were there. There were books by James Oliver Curwood, Gene Stratton Porter, Ben Ames Williams, Harold Bell Wright, Zane Grey, Sinclair Lewis. One old notebook of Mother's had words of the popular songs of the day, written with a fine pen in a careful hand. I explored all of these and read the ones that interested me.

Two trunks filled one corner of the room. We were supposed to stay out of them, but we knew what they contained, along with winter blankets and Dad's blue serge wedding suite and the few mementos of his first wife. Mom's trunk held a few souvenirs of her girlhood and a pair of fancy china vases done in the ornate manner of the Victorian period. These were wedding gifts she never used, either because she didn't like them, or perhaps because she didn't want to see them broken.

Other interesting things were tucked into corners. A kit for developing and printing films, made for use without electricity. I think it belonged to Uncle Bliss, but I never saw it used. An old white metal bed pan always embarrassed me; I hid it in an old straw suitcase so that I would not have to look at it.

My memories of the closet room are mostly pleasant, but one not so pleasant reminds me of the continual problem we had with mice. One hot summer day we began to notice a very unpleasant odor, but could not locate it in the cellar where it was strongest. Finally someone thought of the closet room, which was partly over the cellar stairs, and I went up to investigate. Sure enough, the odor was stronger there, and I soon located it—a family of mice which had died in the old white china pitcher. Holding my nose, I carried it downstairs and outside. The pitcher was never restored to its bowl companion, and was finally broken and thrown away.

There are a few things from that closet room I wish we had carefully saved—pictures of great grandparents that had hung on the wall for years, but had been stored away when the fashion changed and it was no longer popular to have family pictures on the walls; the doll trunk that was made from Dad's small wooden tool chest for my doll Daisy's clothes; and more of the old books.

3

The Old Style Farm Life

The years of the 1920s and 30s are the ones I remember best—from about 1924 when I began school, until I left home in 1936 to work for a year and save money for college. During those years, I was part of the life of the farm, and it seemed a good life, although I always knew I would leave the farm and find my own life in some different place.

Those years were probably the last of the old style of farm life: the years when tractors were taking over from horses, and farmers and their families were beginning to want some of the conveniences for their homes that their town cousins had. The young people realized that college was within their reach, and that they were just as capable as any others anywhere in this country. Our generation knew the old ways of being self-sufficient on a farm, but eagerly adapted to the new.

My sister Evelyn Mae was born on 17 June 1923, ushered into this world by a violent thunderstorm. Lightning struck the house, knocked out the telephone, and burned a streak in the wood siding as it followed the ground wire down the side of the house. After that, Grandpa had lightning rods put on the peaks of the roof and on the big horse barn. We thought they were quite attractive, with their blue glass balls, and one red one.

The spring after Evelyn was born, Grandma was very ill with erysipelas (a skin infection), and I remember seeing her lying in her bed with the high walnut headboard, looking very tiny. The disease especially affected her eyes, and the nurse who came and lived at the farm for a month or six weeks put compresses on them every day.

The nurse was Hilda Holton, recently married to a store owner in Erwin, and her husband, Sid, came to see her every Sunday. The two families became good friends and had a "visiting" friendship as long as my parents lived. They came to the farm for Sunday dinners, and we went to their home in Erwin.

After Grandma was better, Grandpa decided that it was time for her to take life easier, and he decided to buy a house in Bryant. There she would have electric lights and running water and a bathroom with an inside toilet—luxuries she had never had on the farm.

He found a small house with four rooms and a bath, an enclosed front porch, and a coal-and-wood-burning furnace in the basement. They moved in the late summer or early fall. It had just been renovated, but the walls had not yet been painted, and since Grandpa was bothered by the smell of paint, they were not painted as long as Ed and Ida lived there. There was also a garage with a woodshed at one side and an outdoor privy behind it. There was a place at the back for a good-sized garden. The Milwaukee Railroad tracks—the same line that ran through the farm—bordered the back of the garden; the tracks were shielded from sight by a dense lilac hedge.

When Grandma moved to Bryant, she declared that she didn't want to take along the bed with the high walnut headboard—she was tired of dusting it, and anyway, it was too heavy to move again. It was tossed out onto the woodpile, broken up and burned.

Grandma spoke of things that had been left behind when the family moved from Illinois to South Dakota with no regret. I think she had been raised in the pioneer spirit—people kept thinking of moving on west to better land or opportunities, and they left behind the things that would encumber them.

But I have lived long enough to regret that in that move, so many family heirlooms were thrown away. Now I would like to have the pictures of great grandparents that used to hang on the wall of the living room in Grandma's day, and were relegated to the attic when she moved.

The piece I regret losing most was Grandpa's desk, which had interesting pigeonholes and small drawers, and a bookcase with a glass door on the left side. In the bookcase Grandma kept a big book of Bible stories she used to read to us. It had frightening pictures of the flood and Daniel in the lion's den, I remember. There I found Robinson Crusoe, in the original version.

I used to like to look through the little drawers of the desk at the things Grandpa had saved, and I remember especially a postage stamp from the Chicago World's Fair of 1892, and a tiny padlock, which I now have on my charm bracelet.

Grandma did move the pie safe with the punched metal panels to the basement of her new home, and stored jars of fruit and vegetables and laundry soap in it. Years later, when she moved back to the farm again, it was sold or given away. There was no market for things like that in those days.

1924, the year Grandma and Grandpa Ackley moved to town, was also the year I started school—first grade. I went to Erwin Consolidated. The school had flush toilets and drinking fountains and I found a whole new world of friends and books. Here I learned in first grade to read the primer I already knew by heart, and it was a wonderful experience! I rode the four-and-a-half miles to Erwin in the morning and the other eight or ten miles of the route on the way home; the school bus stopped at the end of our driveway every school day for the next 23 years.

My first remembrance of church services centers around a small reed basket which was passed around in the small Sunday School room in the Baptist Church in Bryant. Mrs. Truman, who taught the beginners class, was careful to give different children the honor of passing it each Sunday.

We always had a story, and received a small pamphlet with a Bible story and a corresponding verse to take home. I don't remember a table for handwork, or even coloring pictures, and I suspect that there was no room for such things. But we did sing. I think that was my favorite activity, because I remember especially singing Bringing In The Sheaves with the appropriate arm motions of gathering into our small bosoms the armfuls of sheaves of grain. I liked the rhythm of Count Your Blessings, Name Them One By One, and The Little Brown Church in the Vale.

The small Baptist Church was started by a small group of families who were neither Lutheran nor Roman Catholic, the predominant faiths of most of the community. Many families were first- or second-generation immigrants from the Scandinavian countries or Germany, and there were Lutheran churches which had services in Norwegian, Swedish, German, or Finnish. The Baptist church served the needs of the people who had come from Iowa and

Illinois, who were mostly of Anglo-Saxon origin, and whose families had emigrated much earlier. My Grandfather Griffith was one of the men who started the church, and the names of my aunts and uncles were among the early records.

The Rural Free Delivery meant a great deal to farm families in the early years of this century—probably more than it does now, when every family has some kind of car or truck. One of my earliest memories of Grandpa Ackley, back when he still lived with us at the farm, was of his daily walk to the mailbox, which was about a third of a mile north of the house on the county line road. He would come home with a packet of mail folded inside The Argus Leader, which came from Sioux Falls every morning on the passenger train, and was delivered to our mailbox in the afternoon. When I was old enough to walk that far, I sometimes went with him. After Grandma and Grandpa moved to Bryant, it was my job to get the mail when I was not in school. All the years—until the 1960s, when Uncle Bliss was living on the farm alone—somebody walked to the mailbox in the afternoon.

A daily newspaper has been a part of my day, every day, for most of my life. As soon as I could read for myself, I looked forward to the "funnies" every day. Orphan Annie, Gasoline Alley, and Winnie Winkle were in the comics, the section that I turned to first. In the evenings, I could often persuade my Dad to read the Burgess Bedtime Story of the day. Either the daily paper, or the weekly paper from De Smet or Bryant, used to run serial romantic stories, which gave me the incentive to walk to the mailbox even on a hot summer day.

Even though it was many years ago, my senses remember the feel of the catch on the mailbox, the sound of it opening, and the smell of the newspaper that was folded around whatever we happened to get that day. Sometimes there would be a notice that we had a package, and that we should meet the mailman the next day to receive it. It would usually be clothes or something else from Sears Roebuck or Montgomery Ward. If we expected it to be a large or awkward package, we took the coaster wagon to haul it home, and perhaps a sister to help hold it.

After Grandpa moved to town, he began taking other newspapers, especially the Minneapolis Tribune. I used to persuade him to read me the Uncle Wiggley stories from that paper—the only stories that I remember him reading to me.

When I was only seven or eight, the walk to the mailbox could be a scary walk. I would notice the holes that a badger or skunk had made in the bank at the side of the ditch and hurry past them. When I was a little older, and used to trapping gophers, I was no longer afraid of what might come out of the holes. One time, when the road was newly graded and the ditch a sharp clean cut on the field side, I saw where the entrance had been sliced off a gopher hole. I knew that a short distance inside, the hole would branch into two tunnels, and decided to explore it. I had not reached very far into the entrance when I came upon a nest, and I drew out four tiny, pink, hairless, blind gophers. They looked like mice, except that their heads were bigger. Gophers were pests. I knew that Dad would have killed them, but somehow I couldn't kill those tiny mites of life, and I put them back.

When I was older and had read Gene Stratton Porter's Girl of the Limberlost, I made a butterfly net and took it with me when I went to the mailbox. I made a small collection of the butterflies I caught along the road. I didn't have any books about butterflies, so I didn't learn the names of most of them. I explored the slough alongside the road when it was dry in the fall, and listened to the frogs and watched the red-wing and yellow-headed blackbirds when the slough was full of water.

One late summer day, years later, when I was at home helping with the harvest, I walked to the mailbox with a camera hung round my neck and a .22 rifle over my arm, to see what I could see. I made my way through the dry slough, through willows over my head. When I came out on the far side, there, about 50 feet from me, sat a beautiful red fox. He sat very still, facing me, with his white vest showing off his dark red coat. I stood very still, facing him, and wondering if I should take his picture or shoot him, for I knew that a fox had been stealing chickens around the neighborhood. I did neither, and the magic moment stretched out into perhaps a full minute before he turned and loped off at a leisurely pace across the stubble field.

When Uncle Carl began working for the railroad, he and his family could travel on passes, and they came to the farm to visit. There were just a few times that the entire family gathered at once, but often one parent or the other would come with some of the cousins. Those times when my cousins visited were always special to me. They brought with them the glamour of having traveled all that distance on a train, and I had the luxury of having someone to play with.

My cousin Everett visited the farm with his father when he was six or seven, and stayed on for part of the summer. Another summer both cousins Leslie and Everett stayed with us a month or so. Once we cousins all slept on blankets on the floor, all in a row. I can't remember any quarrels—my memories of those visits were of good times.

Aunt Nellie Ackley came for a visit in June of 1926, bringing cousins Doris, Phyllis, Carol, Arlene, and Jim. This was a mini family reunion, and I remember it with pleasure, although a few pictures of the gathering are probably the best part of my memory. Their visits were all too few, and we didn't get much opportunity to know these cousins.

The Little Things That Matter

Mother's influence began to change the farm in small but important ways after Dad's parents moved to Bryant. She began to raise more chickens, ducks, and geese to sell, and kept more laying hens in order to have more eggs to trade for groceries. She had a brooder house built, and bought an incubator which she kept in the basement. Each spring she hatched a couple of batches of chicks in addition to the chickens, ducks, and geese that were hatched by broody hens.

A mother hen could successfully incubate and hatch five goose eggs, or a few more duck eggs, and she would be a good mother to them until their natural instinct for swimming in puddles or watering troughs took them where she wouldn't go. When this happened, we were always amused at seeing the mother chicken pacing back and forth in great agitation, clucking warnings to them. About that time she usually decided that they were old enough to be on their own, even though they were not ready to abandon the only mother they had ever known. The hen would run determinedly away from them, followed by long-legged, gangly, gray pin-feathered young geese, and they crowded close to her at night when they could no longer creep under her wings.

The extra money from the poultry was Mother's own, and she spent it on extras for her family—clothes, closets for bedrooms, things that couldn't come out of the weekly cream and egg money. When a chick hatchery started up in Bryant, Mom bought registered white Wyandott chicks in order to upgrade her flock and so was able to sell the eggs to the hatchery at premium prices. She no longer hatched eggs in the incubator in the cellar, but bought baby chicks from the hatchery.

Somewhere around 1926, our family joined the millions of others who bought a new kind of entertainment—radio. Our first one was an Atwater Kent with a morning-glory type speaker and three dials for adjusting the tuning. It needed two or three kinds of batteries to supply the power, one of which had to be recharged like a car battery, and we children were not allowed to turn it on ourselves. This was an adult toy!

Dad, especially, enjoyed spending time in the evenings locating different stations and recording the exact setting of all three dials on the cardboard log which he kept. All the stations came in better at night, so in the evenings we could get WLW Cincinnati, KOA Denver, WLS Chicago, a station in Shreveport, Louisiana, and a powerful station at Del Rio, Texas, which had a powerful transmitter across the border in Mexico.

WNAX, Yankton, came in well during the day and the livestock and grain market reports always formed a background to our noon dinner. We listened to many of the popular radio shows—Fibber McGee, Amos n' Andy, Guy Lombardo and his Royal Canadians, Jack Armstrong—and Mother soon learned to enjoy some of the early soap operas that were broadcast in the afternoon, especially Ma Perkins, and Helen Trent.

Later on, during the years of the drought and depression, we had to give up our subscription to the Argus Leader because there was no money for it. It was greatly missed, and was one of the first luxuries the family permitted itself when times got better, along with the telephone, and batteries for the radio.

By 1928, the old Hudson was almost worn out, and Dad and Uncle Bliss bought a new green two-door Chevrolet sedan. We thought it was a wonderful car, but it didn't have the room that the Hudson did, and when all five of us crowded into it to go to town on Saturday night, along with a case of eggs and a can of cream, it was a tight fit.

The man who delivered the new car from an agency in Lake Preston said he would take the old Hudson back with him. We all stood and sadly watched him drive off in it. It didn't run well, and he went roaring down the road in second gear. Years later, when the 1928 Chevrolet gave place to a later model, Dad and my Uncle refused to sell it to a neighbor's son who wanted to buy it for $25. They could not bear the thought of him "running the heart out of it"—the same kind of affection they would have had for an old horse.

I was 11 years old when my youngest sister Dorothy Joan was born, on 18 August 1929, right in the middle of threshing season. We were due to have the threshing crew at our house the next day, and they offered to go to the next farm; but Mother had planned well, and my Aunt Ina and Grandma Griffith and neighbor Stella Coughlin served the dinner to the crew as usual. When I saw my new sister for the first time, with her dark brown hair, she was asleep in an oblong laundry basket painted pale blue.

Our play as young children pantomimed in part the farm life we knew, and one of our favorite games was making playhouses. Evelyn and I could share this even though she was five years younger, though by the time Dorothy was big enough to play, I had outgrown playhouses and they were hers and Evelyn's. For a few happy years Evelyn and I made playhouses with the Coughlin children who lived north of us near our mailbox. There was Geraldine, my age; Dolores, Evelyn's friend; and a younger brother and sister.

We made playhouses under trees, or in an empty bin in the granary, or around a box-like coop we called the goose-house. In early spring the goose-house was home to a couple of geese and their goslings; but by the time we needed it they had moved out. We would define the rooms with pieces of stove wood, or simply with the placement of the "furniture". Again, apple boxes, peach crates, odd boards of all kinds were put to use as furniture, and we saved Mason jar lids, tin cans, Prince Albert tobacco tins, and other cast-offs for our dishes. There were always a few old spoons and pie tins around that added to our household items.

In our play, we mimicked keeping house as we knew it—we "canned" the green pea-like seeds of the asparagus in tobacco tins—and later threw out the foul-smelling mess philosophically. We dug and sifted through a piece of screen brown clay and black loam for sugar and flour and stirred up "cakes" and "cookies" with our flour and water, which we set to bake in our solar oven. We even tried mixing our flour with some of the foam that formed on the pails as the skim milk poured from the separator. We thought this might make an angel-food-like cake, but were disappointed. An occasional stolen egg from the barn made a cake that was different, and it hardened in the sun like a brick!

An outdoor playhouse could adapt itself to any situation. My Griffith grandparents moved to Vienna, South Dakota to operate a gas station there for a few years, and the first house they lived in was next door to a closed flour mill. Grandma soon found that there was some ground grain still in the bottoms of the bins and in the grain chutes, and she got out as much as possible to feed her chickens. Ellwood and I and the boy across the street tried the flour mill residue in making play-house bread, and it browned nicely in the sun, but it smelled bad after a day or two. David Long talked to his parents in sign language, because they were deaf, and that fascinated me. He didn't have a lot of time for play, because his parents needed him.

The plastic toy farms available nowadays reminded me of the miniature farms we used to make on the shady side of the house. Our imagination made pieces of corn cob into different animals, twigs and string made fences, and boxes made barns. We also cut paths and fields, with an old pair of scissors, into the tall jungle of grass in the front yard. This was never a lawn, and we didn't have a lawn mower; it was mowed once or twice in the summer and the grass raked for hay. Most of the fun of these activities was in the making. As I recall, as soon as we had completed them, we were ready to turn to something else.

In the house, when the weather was too cold to play outside, we hung blankets on the clothes line in the south upstairs bedroom and practiced plays, which we wrote ourselves in an old ledger that Grandpa had discarded—plays that were never finished, practiced but never performed for anyone but ourselves and the neighbor girls.

There are lots of places to play and hide on a farm. We "skinned the cat" and hung from our knees, and swung hand over hand from a ladder that was always stored over the alleyway in one of the hog houses. I think we were always practicing for a circus that we planned to give some day. We climbed trees, and played on the gentler-sloping roofs of the cow barn and the old chicken house, and climbed up the grain elevator when it was left beside the granary with one end on the roof.

The Chautauqua was the high point of the summer for the few years it set up tent in Bryant, about 1930, give or take a couple of years. I remember choral programs with a good male chorus, plays (I am sure that one was Gentlemen Prefer Blondes), travel lectures, and instrumental music.

These shows were going on during the summer our cousins Leslie and Everett Ackley spent a month or two with us. We wanted season tickets, and for this special privilege we had to earn the money. Dad decided that a good project would be for us to trap gophers.

Pocket gophers invaded the alfalfa field and ate the roots, and striped gophers and flickertails made holes in the pasture. Flickertails and striped gophers can be trapped with the old familiar traps or snares, but pocket gophers are more like moles, and difficult to trap. They live completely underground, but leave a trail of mounds of earth from digging their tunnels.

Dad bought (I think from Sears Roebuck) half a dozen traps called "death clutch", and we learned how to set them in the holes. We would probe in a mound of earth until we found the tunnel, where the gopher had packed the entrance full of dirt. Then we dug it out, set the trap in the tunnel entrance, and pegged it to the ground with a wooden stick. We needed no bait—the light in the tunnel would bring the gopher to investigate, and it would be caught between the two sharp prongs that closed in from the sides.

We were two teams—Leslie and Evelyn, Everett and I—and we split the dime we earned for each gopher. We caught enough of the little brown pests to pay the $2.00 for a season ticket that summer—probably five shows.

The Baptist Church in Bryant was no longer able to keep going because of dwindling membership, and the church was closed. Grandma became trustee of the property, and we used to like to go with her when she went to check out the empty building. She became a regular in attendance at the Congregational Church, a block from her home, and taught the Bible Class there as long as she was able.

When Dorothy was in high school, she and Evelyn and I joined the Congregational Church together. Our parents joined later; it was harder for them to give up their Baptist heritage.

Some of my fondest memories connected with both of these churches were of the Christmas programs. I remember learning a poem or song called Hang Up The Baby's Stocking to perform in a program when I was about four years old, and singing it while rocking in a small rocker on the platform. I don't remember being shy or frightened.

One Christmas both my cousin Quentin Houge and I received Lee overall dolls from the hands of Santa who took them off the Christmas tree. Grandma Griffith had placed them there for us. That was at the Baptist Church. At the Congregational Church we always had a Christmas tree and Santa Claus handed out boxes or bags of candy, although some lucky children got real presents from the tree.

One Christmas Eve, when I must have been in 6th or 7th grade, it started to snow late in the afternoon, and we knew that we could never get to town in the car. Dad was all for staying at home and forgetting the program, but we girls were so disappointed that he finally hitched up a team. We bundled up in warm clothes and went to town in the bob-sled. It had taken a while to persuade Dad to go, and of course we were late, but we did arrive in time to take our parts in the program and receive our treats from Santa.

In the early 1930s, Grandpa began to lose his eyesight to cataracts, and it was a great trial to him. One of his greatest pleasures had always been reading, and as his sight dimmed, he could read less and less. Dad took him to an eye specialist in Sioux Falls who said that the cataracts could be removed to restore his sight. "If he were my father," he said, "he would not have those another day!" But Grandpa would not have an operation. We never could figure out why he refused, when he was so handicapped without sight.

Grandpa had never wanted a radio because there wasn't much that he wanted to listen to, but now that seemed to be the best solution. There just wasn't any money to buy him one.

I'm not sure whose idea it was—probably not ours—for Evelyn and me to take money from our bank savings accounts to buy him the radio, but we readily agreed. We each contributed $12.50 toward the $25 table model. I think it was a Crosley. It had an arch-shaped top and simple controls.

Grandpa soon learned to find his favorite stations and the times they broadcast news. There were never enough news and serious programs to satisfy him, and he didn't care much for music, but he rather enjoyed the radio. It also relieved Grandma of the chore of reading all of the daily paper to him, but he still had to have someone read him the editorials. When we went to town on Saturday afternoons, I was often pressed into service, and so was Evelyn, when she was old enough. I remember sitting on the small front porch reading editorials in the summertime when I would so much rather have been doing something else!

As far as I am aware, from the years 1917 to 1921, the family had no dogs. In 1921, when I was four, we got Bingo, who was my pet. We had Bingo only one summer, however, because he soon learned that it was fun to chase chickens and ducks, and even kill the little ones, and Dad had to shoot him. A few years later, Buster met the same fate for the same reason.

Several more years passed without a dog, and then we got Tyke, named by Uncle Bliss with the nickname he had given me when I was little. Tyke was a small black and white fox terrier, who was so tiny when we got him that he was like a kitten. My little sister Dorothy was not afraid of him, and so got over her great fear of dogs. Tyke earned his keep by killing rats and mice, and even a weasel that had taken up residence under the "barley house", a single grain bin near the hog pen which was always used to store barley for hog feed. Tyke was such a good dog and so well-behaved that he was allowed to be in the house. I don't remember what finally happened to him.

Dad had always admired collies, and about 1936 or 1937 he ordered a spayed female collie, which we named Lassie—what else? Lassie was a farm pet, loved by all, and she lived out her long life there, 18 years. After Dorothy and Harold married and lived on the farm, Harold's dog, Pat, came to live on the farm and lived there the rest of his life, staying with Lassie and Uncle Bliss when Dorothy and Harold moved to a farm of their own.

Once I had a pet rooster—also called Bingo. He followed me around the farm and waited for me to turn over rocks so that he could catch the crickets that were underneath. That Bingo met a tragic end when a horse stepped on him in the barn.

We always had cats, sometimes as many as 25, and of course feeding them was a problem. Mostly they fed themselves, on rats and mice and gophers, with milk in the mornings and evenings when the cows were milked. After the morning milking, the men would usually pour a little warm milk into a pan in the cow barn for the cats. These cats were not allowed in the house, and were mostly quite wild, although Dad liked cats and always had one or two tamed for his pets.

Mother recalled that one of Dad's favorite cats was in the house one day and made a mess in the middle of their bed in the upstairs bedroom. After that, the cats were banished from the house, though there was usually one tame enough to sit hopefully on the steps by the back door. That one tame cat was often an orange or butterscotch color, and usually answered to the name of "Kitty Buff" when I was small.

Later on, the tame cat was always "Tom", and I remember one Tom that was black and fluffy. Tom was usually tame enough so that he would sit up on his haunches in the cow barn at milking time and wait for Dad to squirt milk directly from the cow's teat into his mouth. When he had had enough, he would walk away to wash his face and whiskers. The other cats, not so confident of their place, sat back and waited for Dad to pour some milk into their pans. They didn't get much fresh whole milk, but in the evenings, after the milk was separated, Dad would come back with skim milk to feed the calves, and the cats always got a generous panful, complete with foam on top.

We never did much about having the cats vaccinated for distemper, and some years nearly all of them would die of the disease. I remember one time that there were so few cats that Dad and Uncle Bliss had to resort to trying to poison the rats, whose population went much greater when there were no cats to kill the young ones. The cats probably never tangled with a full-grown rat, which could be a formidable opponent.

Some of the cats had distinct personalities, and we noticed them, but mostly they were just part of the gang. In times of a cat shortage, Dad would try to protect the newborn kittens from the toms, who might kill them, especially a tom from another farm. One slim, very young female that I remember seemed to be protesting motherhood at too tender an age—she carried her kittens out into the middle of the yard and left them there, abandoning them to die or be killed.

We used to try to find nests of new kittens and play with them enough to tame them, but as soon as they were partly grown they hissed and clawed when we picked them up.

In his last years, Uncle Bliss, who was also fond of cats, bought cat food for the several cats that remained.

I always thought that I grew up in one of the backwaters of the United States, until one day I was talking about childhood experiences with a friend who grew up in Cincinnati. After I had related how I had once skipped riding home on the school bus to take the train to Bryant, seven miles away, to stay overnight with my grandparents, she said, "Do you know I never rode on a train until I was a Girl Scout leader and took my troop to Chattanooga? I lived in a city all my life and we never went anywhere, except to visit relatives in the city."

That set me to thinking, and I realized that, in retrospect, although we did live in a rural, off-the-beaten-path part of the country, we reached out to the rest of the country. We had newspapers, magazines, and radio and felt that we were a part of the whole. We knew that we had to get more education so that we wouldn't have to stay there if we didn't want to, and the future was open to us. Many of us left for other parts of the country where jobs were more plentiful, but we were always proud of our heritage, and often went back to our roots.

5

Visiting and Visitors

We always looked forward to visitors on the farm, and we didn't have too many. We didn't often go visiting on Sundays, because Dad was tired from a week's work in the fields, and he welcomed a chance to take a Sunday afternoon nap.

But some Sundays during the summer, when I was small, we went to dinner at Grandma and Grandpa Griffith's in Bryant. The first gatherings I remember there often included cousins and aunts and uncles—Mother's married sisters and brothers and their families. There were so many people that they would have two table settings. I can't remember what age groups got to eat first, but I think they fed the kids first so the elders could linger around the table over coffee.

As more grandchildren were added, and the grandparents grew older, these family dinners became too much work, and were reluctantly stopped. Old pictures of gatherings of Mother's family show that they were a regular part of summer Sundays.

Sometimes we made a trip to the farm home of Mother's sister Ruth and her husband Uncle John Haney, near Watertown—a full day's excursion—for Sunday dinner, and we always enjoyed that; they came to visit us in summer or fall, too. We visited Mom's brother Victor's family in Vienna. Another of Mom's sisters, Aunt Maggie Houge, made the best ice cream I ever ate and she liked to experiment with different flavors and recipes. They ran a dairy and so had plenty of good cream.

On Saturdays we liked especially to stop in at Grandma Griffith's, because that day she usually baked bread. We ate fresh-from-the-oven kropfuls—raised doughnuts filled with jelly—or apple kuchen made with cinnamon-flavored sour cream over apple slices.

Mother's youngest brother, Elwood Griffith, was only two years older than I, and he became the brother we never had. He stayed at the farm often—as often as we could arrange it. I had a canvas pup tent; it was one of our favorite playthings in the summer. We put it up, took it down and moved it to another spot in my wagon, and put it up again. My doll Daisy and her trunk of clothes went along, and the tent was a prop for many different kinds of play. When we lost the original wooden pegs, we whittled out some new ones from the thicker ends of peach crates and apple boxes. My tool was the draw-knife, and I could make dandy tent pegs with it!

We climbed on the gentler-sloping roofs of some of the barns, played in the haymow, helped with the chores. Elwood (called "Buz" when we were small) was always handy with tools; he even made a two-wheeled trailer out of my little wooden wagon after Uncle Bliss backed into it with the car. After that accident, Uncle Bliss came home one day with a bright red metal coaster wagon. We could hitch the wooden trailer onto the back of the new wagon and haul the tent, doll, tea set—all kinds of things around in it. The red wagon eventually lost its bright red paint, but it was useful on the farm almost as long as anyone lived there.

When we had an uncle-brother or boy cousins to play with, we learned to play Indians and Cops and Robbers. We made guns by whittling a gun-shape from the end of a peach crate with a snap clothespin fastened to the back. The ammunition was rubber bands cut from an old tire inner tube, stretched around the "barrel" of the gun and held with the clothespin. Sometimes we made rifles the same way and looped several rubber bands together for the ammunition. The sting from one of those projectiles was enough to make a lively game of Cops and Robbers. This was the era of gangsters, and we played the incidents we heard about on the news.

Another type of "weapon" that we learned to make was a sling to shoot arrows. I don't think we knew that this was a very ancient type of weapon. The arrows were cut from odd pieces of wooden shingles, just a long slim sliver about three eighths of an inch thick, with a notch cut near the thicker end. The sling was simply a stick with a knotted string attached. We slipped the knot into the notch of the arrow and propelled it with a sweep of an arm. We didn't try to shoot each other with those—mostly we tried to see how high or how far we could shoot the arrow, the favorite feat being to shoot it over the radio aerial that was connected to the barn.

Saturday night in town was the highlight of our week, and it gave everyone in the family something special. We would try to get to town early enough so that we could park the car on either side of the one main block of stores, but usually we were too late—the townspeople often took their car uptown and parked it in front of Hestad's General Store or Baumbach's Cafe or Fairchild's Drugstore before supper; then they left it there for a grandstand seat for people-watching later in the evening. We girls usually found friends to visit with or to walk around with, and always hoped to find friends or relatives in a well-placed car when we got tired of walking around the block.

Mom would sell the eggs, make her grocery purchases for the week if she hadn't already gone to town to do that in the afternoon, and then she would look for a friend in a car or her sister Maggie to sit and visit with. Dad and Uncle Bliss went to the hardware store and the grain elevator office and the lumber yard, where they found friends to talk with.

We looked forward to going to the movies—which cost 10¢ or 15¢ for children—and that was the most worldly of our entertainments. The shows we saw then needed no parental permission. We were delighted with the first of the color films, especially Al Jolson and the musicals.

When we were all gathered together for the ride home, we were always pleased when Dad would say, "Let's go and have a dish of ice cream!" And then we would all go to Baumbach's Cafe, sit in a booth, and have ice cream in a dish with a paper cone inside—maybe even a sundae!

When fall came and it was too cold to stand around or sit in cars, we were likely to go to a movie and go home earlier. While Grandma and Grandpa Ackley lived in town, we would spend part of the evening with them. If the Saturday trip had to be made in a wagon or bobsled because of snow or bad roads, we went in the afternoon and stayed home to listen to the radio that night.

If I couldn't find a friend to visit with, I might go to Kelly and Gilbertson's Hardware store, where Mrs. Gilbertson always had a stack of National Geographic issues handy near the pot-bellied stove for people to sit around and look at.

After Bryant High School started a school band, there were sometimes concerts on Saturday night. Mom's brother Elwood played in it, as did my cousin Quentin Houge.

Once every summer Bryant had a festival, usually called a "celebration". Then the block or two of Main Street would be closed to vehicles and reserved for a merry-go-round, ferris wheel, and other rides, as well as games of chance—"Hit the target and win a Cupie doll!" There were all of the carnival stands—the Egyptian exotic dancers, the weight-guessing stand, and popcorn, cotton candy, and hot dogs. I remember my first ride on a ferris wheel. Uncle Bliss decided to take me to the carnival one night when the rest of the family didn't go. I wanted to ride the ferris wheel, and was perfectly willing to go alone. He didn't want to ride, but he couldn't let me go alone, so he braved the height and motion of the ride. I thought it was great, but Uncle Bliss was much relieved when we got off.

A circus came to Bryant during several summers in the late 1920s. The small, one-ring shows held as much excitement for us as the Ringling Brothers and Barnum & Bailey three-ring extravaganza ever has in later years. They always set up their tents in the grass of the park across the railroad tracks from Grandma Ackley's house. There would be one large tent with small ones around it that housed the side shows. We weren't usually allowed to go into the side shows, but I remember seeing the bearded lady, the fat lady, and a two-headed calf. The trapeze artists, the clowns, the elephants and ponies were all colorful and exciting—the same as a circus today, only in miniature. One time I saw what was supposed to be the mummified body of John Wilkes Booth, but I don't remember if that was at a circus or a carnival.

The Chautauqua Movement must have been in its last years of providing lectures, concerts, and drama across the midwest when my cousins and I went to the summer programs they sponsored in Bryant. I remember sitting on benches or wooden chairs under a large tent, with grass underfoot, watching a magician, choral groups, and plays.

One magician I remember—not the man, but his program—did wonderful tricks with scarves of many colors coming out of a tube. He found coins behind the ears of unsuspecting boys in the audience, and pulled the exact card a woman had chosen out of a deck. He sawed his pretty girl assistant in half and then presented her, whole, to the audience. To me, most amazing and memorable of all was his small troop of trained white pigeons. They performed in and around a stage prop like a dollhouse for pigeons. The finale of their act was putting out a small flaming fire in their house. I think they carried tiny buckets of water in their bills!

One of our annual gatherings at the farm started as a celebration of a successful partnership between neighbors. For many years, the corn for cattle and hog feed was picked by hand, after the stalks and ears had dried. The picker could usually fill a triple-box wagon in half a day—two loads a day. In the late 1920s, Dad bought a one-row, horse drawn mechanical picker in partnership with our neighbor, John Hinder and his son Harm. The first year that they owned it, they were so pleased with getting the corn picked so quickly and easily that they wanted to celebrate with a special feast. Dad and Harm picked the menu—oyster stew and home-made ice cream! This celebration came to be repeated every fall, and was always held at our house, as long as the two families owned the corn picker.

We always enjoyed gatherings of neighbors—in the winter for card parties and dances, in summer for picnics.

One of our neighbors was Jim Colburn, who lived with his wife Josie and his elderly father (who was the only Civil War veteran living in our area) on the banks of Colburn Lake, or Plum Lake, about two-and-a-half miles from the farm. Jim played a lively old-time fiddle, also banjo and mandolin, and he loved to play and see people dance. Ed Coughlom loved to dance, but his specialty was calling square dances. (Some people insisted that they had heard him practicing while working with a team of horses in a field.)

One young married couple, Hank and Marie Hinders, lived in a farm house with an extra large kitchen, and they enjoyed the gatherings so much that we always had the dances at their house. With care, we could fit two squares of dancers into the room. Everyone danced with everyone, and it was there I learned some of the old "play party" dances (called round dances now) and some of the old-time squares. "Skip-To-My Lou" for instance, was an old round dance from colonial times.

There was usually a game of whist going on in the corner of the living room at any neighborhood party, and a group of women who either visited, played cards, or danced. Babies fell asleep among the coats piled on a bed in the bedroom. The young people played games or danced, depending on whose home we were in. Mom never learned to dance because her father wouldn't allow it, but Dad had danced as a young unmarried man in the "ballroom" above Ward's Store in Bryant. One of my best memories of these parties was of the few times that I waltzed with my Dad.

In the busy summer, we welcomed any diversion. We never took a vacation trip, and the best we girls could hope for was a church picnic on a Sunday at Lake Norden or a Sunday visit with relatives.

Neighborhood picnics in the summer came to be a part of our social life, and I think these were an outgrowth of the Extension Club which Mom helped to organize in the late 1920s. The farm women enjoyed their club meetings with the "lessons" in sewing, cooking, home decorating, and gardening, and it was easy to find special occasions for family picnics.

Our family could borrow the five-gallon ice cream freezer that belonged to the old Baptist Church, and we always froze it full of ice cream for a picnic. Usually every family brought eggs, cream, milk, and flavorings to fill the freezer, and it was part of the fun of the gathering to mix and freeze it. There were plenty of young people to take turns turning the crank (on that large freezer, it was a flywheel) for a chance to lick the paddle. Someone had to go to town for several blocks of ice and bring them back in tubs covered with horse blankets. We had a gallon-sized freezer; another family a six-quart-sized freezer. Often all were used—and no ice cream ever went to waste!

After the ice cream was frozen, it was packed with more ice and salt, to season for a couple of hours. The company separated into age groups to visit, play cards, perhaps have a ball game or a game of hide-and-seek around the farm buildings. We all gathered again for a supper of sandwiches, potato salad, baked beans, and pickles, and finished with ice cream and cake.

The Fourth-of-July fireworks I remember were always at home. I suppose this was because the picnic broke up when everyone had to go home to do the chores and milk the cows. Dad liked to have fireworks to set off in the front yard. Sometimes a neighbor family or two would join us and add their fireworks to ours for a more impressive display. Dad always had a pinwheel which he fastened onto the telephone pole in the front yard, and we had Roman candles and sky rockets, "snakes" and some larger crackers placed under cans. We children had the tiny firecrackers, which were fastened together with their braided fuses, and we always had sparklers to hold in our hands and wave in the air.

6

Times of Plenty

Except for the drought years, we always had plenty to eat on the farm, even if we had a lot of snow and storms. In winter we ate mostly canned vegetables and potatoes with either fresh meat, if the weather was cold enough to keep it frozen, or chicken, or the last of the summer's ham and bacon. The cellar held 30 or so bushels of potatoes, carrots in a jar of sand, a few Hubbard squash, onions, and many quart jars of vegetables and fruit. We canned peas and corn and green beans, beets and beet greens and several kinds of pickles, hominy, and sauerkraut. We had peaches and pears and strawberries, apricots and cherries and rhubarb. Apples were bought fresh, by the crate, all winter long.

Each year, on one day in the fall, when Dad had taken a load of grain to the elevator in town, he would come home with 10 or 12 fifty-pound sacks of flour and a sack of sugar—our winter supply. He and Uncle Bliss would carry these sacks upstairs to the small hallway under the eaves at the head of the stairs, where they were stored. The sugar, in a muslin bag inside a burlap bag, was stored there, too.

For several years Dad ordered 100 pounds of frozen fish from Minnesota, always counting on having weather cold enough to keep it frozen. He would get an assortment of different kinds; and I was always glad when we found a female full of eggs—we knew nothing of caviar then, but they were good fried.

Noon was dinner time—the big meal of the day, especially in summer. We always had potatoes and meat, a vegetable or two, or salad, bread and butter, and dessert, often pudding or pie. I remember making chocolate or butterscotch pudding and carefully measuring it out by spoonfuls into six dessert dishes—we were all equal there.

Sunday dinner was usually a little more special, the main dish a beef or pork roast in season or chicken and noodles in winter. In summer we looked forward to having the first meal of fried chicken, but Mom wouldn't use the young fryers until they weighed five pounds. She felt it was wasteful to eat them when they were smaller than that. Another favorite meal was a boiled dinner featuring either beef, or the last of a ham with potatoes, onions, carrots, and cabbage. Mom usually made her own noodles; she rolled them thin, laid them out on towels to dry, and then sliced them into strips about two inches long and a quarter of an inch wide.

Winter meals were not as hearty as those in summer, and our noon dinner would often be vegetable or bean or potato soup, or a one-dish meal like a spaghetti casserole. Mom made what she called "chili con carne" which consisted of hamburger, kidney beans, onions, tomatoes, and corn. Or we might have waffles or pancakes with fresh brown sugar syrup.

Breakfast in winter was often oatmeal, or cornmeal mush, with real cream and brown sugar. Or it might be eggs and bacon, perhaps fried potatoes. The heavier breakfasts were really summer fare, when the men had been up early to milk cows and do other chores for a couple of hours before coming in to eat. We all liked milk toast, which Mom made by toasting slices of bread over the coals of the wood fire and then covering them with milk and cream in a kettle. We ate it in bowls like cereal. Some days we had whole wheat pancakes, with brown sugar syrup. Usually in winter we had grapefruit or oranges, and everyone dug the sections out with an orange spoon. Never did we have juice. Summer breakfasts were much the same, except that the cereal might be cornflakes.

Holidays were usually celebrated with a special meal. Thanksgiving and Christmas featured roast goose or duck, sometimes turkey, or even a beef roast. I remember having celery or head lettuce, store-bought, on these special occasions. We had cranberry sauce, too, always the cooked kind, and possibly fruit jello with whipped cream. Pies were often holiday desserts—apple, rhubarb in the spring, raisin, mincemeat (homemade mincemeat made with goose meat), and a special strawberry pie made with a quart of strawberries in a baked pie shell, covered with a recipe of seven-minute icing. The icing trickled down through the berries and sweetened them.

Our evening meal was supper, and we usually had some leftovers from noon. We planned leftover potatoes when we peeled them for noon dinner, and they would be fried or creamed for supper. We usually had meat or cheese, fresh hamburger or weiners or cold cuts if someone had been to town in the afternoon. Supper was the time for fruit—fresh or canned, depending on the season. That was when we had cake, too, for dessert. Cookies were for whenever you were hungry! Mom bought peaches, apricots, white seedless grapes, and sometimes strawberries and raspberries by the crate and canned them. But we always ate as much as we wanted of the fresh fruit, too.

Sunday supper in the wintertime was sometimes popcorn, and a bowl or cup of hot milk. That was good with a chunk of butter and maybe a little sugar added, and some bread—hot bread and milk.

When someone went to town in the afternoon in the summertime, she or he usually came home with meat for supper—a change from whatever we had been eating. Fresh hamburger was always a treat after many meals of ham or bacon or canned sausage. I always liked to go along to the butcher shop, because Mr. Dyson would always give me a weiner to eat right there in the shop.

Dad liked to hunt, pheasants in the fall after harvest and ducks a little later. I remember seeing Mom plucking ducks and saving the down for pillows, although she probably filled more pillows with down from domestic ducks and geese. Dad never shot deer because when I was growing up there weren't any in our part of the state. It was only years later, when more trees had been planted, that the deer found their way into eastern South Dakota.

When the pigeons got too thick around the barns, Dad would decide that it was time for pigeon pie. He would feed them corn in the middle of the yard for several days until they were used to finding it there. Then he would put corn in a small area to concentrate his flock, and shoot into the pile-up of birds with a shotgun. A dozen or fifteen pigeons made a plentiful roasterful, and, baked in their own gravy and topped with biscuits, they made a good meal! There wasn't much meat on a pigeon, but the breast and legs of a dozen of them were plenty.

Dad hunted cottontail rabbits, too, until they developed a disease that made them unsafe to skin. He always skinned the rabbits, I remember, but it fell to Mother to pluck ducks, skin pheasants, and scale fish.

We raised chickens and ducks and geese, and ate some of all of them. One year we had turkeys, but they were too susceptible to disease, especially when raised near other poultry, and Mom didn't want to bother with them. We had guinea hens for a few years, and they were good "watch dogs", as good as geese. Their meat was all dark and very good. Guineas didn't like to be cooped up, and would nest in the grass or the shelterbelt, and that was what finally finished them off—foxes or other wild animals found the nests.

(During the drought, for the year or two that Dad was on WPA, the federal Works Progress Administration, and hauled gravel for roads, we got "commodities". I remember canned vegetables that weren't as good as what we canned ourselves, and cans of meat and sacks of flour. The vegetables were all right, but the canned meat was mutton, and there was no way Mom could disguise the smell when she opened a can to make stew! You could smell it everywhere in the house, and it was years before we could appreciate roast lamb or lamb chops.)

When the men were not home at noon, during threshing time for example, Mom would fix for us things that Dad didn't like: melted cheese that we ate on bread (more like today's fried cheese) or potato pancakes made with grated raw potato.

Sometimes instead of making cottage cheese, Mom would make a soft cheese she called smear kase (spread cheese) by aging the curds for a few days, then cooking them with cream, salt and pepper, and pouring it in a mold to cool. Except for Camembert or Brie, I have never found any other cheese similar to it.

One favorite wintertime supper was what we called a "butterfly supper"—it was baked potatoes and baked squash, and it made the butter fly! No baked potatoes or Hubbard squash has ever tasted so good as that! The potatoes would come out of the oven with crisp skins and mealy centers, and the squash the same. I can picture the scene now—the kitchen on a dark winter night lighted only by a kerosene lamp with a reflector behind it, Dad and Uncle Bliss coming in from feeding the calves and hanging their caps and jackets by the stove, and a big platter of potatoes and squash ready to be set on the table.

I learned to bake bread when I was about 14, and only one time did I ever have a spoiled batch. Mom and Dad had gone to visit my aunts in Waterloo, Iowa, for about a week, and the first batch of bread that I tried while they were gone spoiled overnight in the sponge stage. I took it out in the garden, dug a hole, and buried it—and swore my sisters to secrecy.

I cannot remember an exact recipe for bread. We started with potato water from boiled potatoes, with a mashed potato and some sugar added to the mixture. When this had cooled to lukewarm, one or two cakes of yeast were added, and enough flour to make a soft batter. This was placed in a large pan and left on top of the kitchen range until the next morning. The brand of yeast we used was called Yeast Foam, and it looked like squares of dry cornmeal.

By the next morning the mixture was foamy and lively. We stirred more flour into it, added a little shortening, and turned out the dough onto the cabinet surface in the pantry to knead. That was the fun part. I learned by doing, and I have always liked the feel of kneading bread. It felt alive, and it responded to the touch of my hands. After kneading, it was set to rise, then punched down to rise again, and finally divided into four large loaves. While these loaves were rising, the wood fire in the kitchen stove was built up to make the oven temperature just right for baking. That was the trickiest part of bread baking; it was easy to have it too hot. We usually baked bread twice a week, and it was good bread, light and crusty. Sometimes we made cinnamon rolls from part of the dough. We enjoyed the change, however, when Mom bought a loaf or two at the bakery in town.

In summer, any cooking after our noon dinner was done on the three-burner kerosene stove in the pantry. The pantry housed the kerosene stove, some shelving, the DeLaval cream separator, and a kitchen cabinet that was a marvelous baking center and storage cabinet.

The kitchen cabinet was one of those which are coveted now by collectors—it held a flour bin which had a sifter in the bottom, and, if memory serves, it could hold a whole 50-lb. sack of flour, and dispense it, already sifted, into a cup. When we wanted flour, we turned the crank and held a cup under the sifter. Most recipes of those days called for sifted flour—this was before the days of pre-sifted. The bin could be lowered on hinged holders in order to be filled with flour.

We mixed bread on the cabinet's enameled counter, and stored the baked bread in a tin-lined drawer. Pots and pans and bowls and kitchen knives were all stored in its drawers and spaces.

Here we mixed the dozens of cookies that were almost always on hand. Dad liked cookies for snacking, and when the two large tin cans—one round and one square-sided—that sat on a shelf in the pantry were empty, we refilled them. The cans stood perhaps 15 inches tall, and when we baked cookies, we usually made two kinds, one for each can. We baked sugar cookies, sandwich cookies made of two rolled circles filled with raisin filling, soft ginger cookies with white frosting, oatmeal raisin cookies, and peanut butter cookies. Another favorite was called "Rocks", containing raisins and nuts. And at butchering time, we sometimes made crackling cookies—a spice cookie with bits of meat like crumbled bacon. I don't remember that chocolate cookies were made very often, and there were no chocolate chips in those days.

VERNA ACKLEY'S PEANUT BUTTER COOKIES

1 cup brown sugar
1 cup white sugar
1 cup shortening
1 cup peanut butter (either smooth or crunchy)
2 eggs well beaten
1/2 teaspoon salt
2 level teaspoons soda, sifted with
3 cups flour.

Cream shortening and sugars until fluffy. Add peanut butter and eggs and salt. Gradually add the flour-soda mixture to make a stiff dough. Roll in balls and place on ungreased cookie sheet. Flatten with a fork dipped in flour. Bake at 375°10-12 minutes.

(In the years that I baked cookies for hungry kids, I tried pressing the dough into two jelly-roll pans, sprinkling with sugar, and baking about 15 minutes. When done, I cut them into bars.)

Part of the time, we churned our own butter in a wooden churn. The butter would be "worked" (that is, all the liquid worked out of it) in a wooden bowl with a wooden paddle. Then it would be salted and packed into stone crocks. When we began to sell cream to the Lake Norden Creamery, we could also buy butter from the truck when it made its rounds. We also had a small glass churn which held a couple of gallons of cream, and we often made our own butter in this "Daisy" churn.

One summer Dad decided to try making his own root beer. He had read an ad with the directions and decided that it wouldn't be too hard. It required a bottle of the extract, some yeast and sugar, and of course, water. We had 5- and 10-gallon cream cans to brew it in, but we had to buy a bottle capper, caps, and bottles. Dad mixed the ingredients in the large cream can, and we waited impatiently for it to "work" a little before it could be bottled. It turned out well, so for the next several years, Dad made root beer in the summertime. When we wanted a refreshing treat, say in the evening after a hot day's work, we put several bottles in the bucket over the water tank near the barn, where the coldest water from the well would trickle over it. With no refrigeration, this was the coldest we could get it. It tasted good and refreshing.

We didn't have pop very often, but Grandpa Griffith, who ran a gas station and garage in Bryant, sold pop. When I stayed there, the rule was one bottle a day. Usually we all enjoyed a bottle of grape Nehi or orange soda in the evening when we would sit in the wooden swing which was hung between two trees on the lawn beside the station. It was a good place to sit on Saturday night when everyone came to town—people would wave or call a greeting, or even stop for gas.

ROCKS

1 cup soft shortening (half butter), I think we used lard.
1-1/2 cups brown sugar
3 eggs
2 tsp cinnamon
3 cups flour
1 cup seedless raisins
1 tsp soda
1 cup chopped nuts
1/2 tsp salt

Heat oven to 375°. Mix shortening, sugar and eggs thoroughly. Blend dry ingredients and stir in. Mix in raisins and nuts. Drop by rounded teaspoonfuls 2" apart onto greased baking sheet, and bake 8-10 minutes. Makes about 5 dozen cookies.

Prairie Land

Prairie land, flat land,
Seared brown by the relentless sun.
Big tractors plow and harrow
To plant the flat land.
Dust devils dance up and down the fields.
Fragile green spears burst forth
From dark fresh-turned ground.

If the snow falls,
If the rains come
It is never much west of the hundredth,
But there will be harvest.
Wheat will fill the hopper cars
Standing on the siding
To make the world's bread.

— 1970s, Evelyn Ackley Christensen (1923-2006)

Photographs

NOTE: All photos are by Helen Ruth Ackley Johnson unless otherwise credited.

Edward Everett and Mary Ida (Maxwell) Ackley at the time of their wedding, 1883. Family photograph.

Leslie, Edward, Ida, and Bliss Ackley, ca. 1930. Family photograph.

Snow covering corn cribs, woodpile, old engine, ca. 1920. Family photograph.

Leslie on triple-box wagon, with horses King and Florrie, ca. 1920. Family photograph.

Edward and Bliss on binders, ca. 1920. Family photograph.

Leslie Ackley, Heironymous (last name unknown), Edward Ackley, and John Hinders with the spring butchering, ca. 1920. Family photograph.

LEFT: Lifting hay into the haymow of the horse barn, ca. 1920. Family photograph.

RIGHT: Nellie Ackley, Ida Ackley, and Verna (Griffith) Ackley, ca. 1916.
Family photograph.

The farmhouse with Helen on the front porch, ca. 1922. Family photograph.

One of the original green school buses, purchased in 1923. Family photograph.

Helen with visiting cousins in the old Hudson, ca. 1923. Family photograph.

Elevating grain into the granary, ca. 1940. Family photograph.

The farm from the air, 1942. Family photograph.

The growing family: (Back row) Harold Sauder, Ed Christensen, Verna
Ackley, Helen and Edwin Johnson, (Front row) Dorothy Ackley Sauder,
Evelyn Ackley Christensen, Helen's daughter Linda (on Grandma Ackley's
lap), and Leslie Ackley, 1949. Family photograph.

The farm windmill over a 250-foot-deep well, 1942. Helen used to climb it all the way to the top.

The steam engine, ca. 1940.

Threshing grain with the old-fashioned steam engine, ca. 1942.

Evelyn on the binder, ca. 1942.

Leslie plowing with the old John Deere and a three-bottom plow, ca. 1942.

Leslie harvesting grain, ca. 1942.

The first task in the morning. Leslie greases the binder, ca. 1942.

Amber durum wheat against a blue South Dakota sky, ca. 1942.

A pile of straw bales, ca. 1942.

Threshing grain, ca. 1942.

Uncle Bliss shocking wheat, ca. 1942.

Bliss and Leslie stacking alfalfa hay, ca. 1942.

Verna driving a team on the "buck rake" to move hay to the stack, ca. 1942.

Verna with her chickens, ca. 1941.

Pheasant hunting: Paul Vincent, Frank Johnson, and a friend, 1945.

Farm neighbors on a pheasant hunt, 1945.

Bliss and Edwin with the new tractor, ca. 1940.

Leslie, ca. 1942.

Dorothy, ca. 1942.

Helen, self portrait, ca. 1945.

Lunch break near the threshing machine, ca. 1941.

Threshing. Leslie (center) and the neighbors survey the flax, ca. 1942.

A gallon pail wrapped in wet newspaper provides a cool drink, ca. 1942.

Leslie harvesting potatoes with a potato digger, ca. 1940.

Leslie with Lassie; Verna on the rake in the background, ca. 1940.

Uncle Bliss, ca. 1940.

This photo, taken by Helen, of the 1949 Ford was a finalist in the first Smithsonian Magazine photo contest, and was published in the June 2004 magazine when Helen was in hospice at age 86.

"Ballet" frozen overalls on the clothesline, ca. 1942.

The farm in winter, ca. 1946.

Leslie and Verna, ca. 1942.

Edwin Elliott Johnson, ca. 1942.

Edwin Elliott Johnson, ca. 1942.

Helen and Edwin, ca. 1942. Photo by Edwin E. Johnson.

Helen Ruth Ackley Johnson. Photos by Edwin E. Johnson.

Milkweed pod in autumn, ca. 1942.

Helen Ruth Ackley Johnson at the turn of the new century. Photographer unknown.

7

Prairie Pastures and Pens

The farm depended on horse power.

Horses are a little like children. They have different personalities; they are creatures of habit; some work well with others; some pick on others or fight. I don't know how many horses came from Illinois in the "immigrant car", but it was soon necessary to buy more. Dad and Uncle Carl were old enough to work in the fields when school was out, and Uncle Bliss, too, had finished Ag School by 1916 or 1917.

Grandpa had a new horse barn built big enough for 12 or even 14 horses, and had it painted barn red. It must have been good paint—I don't remember it ever being repainted. I always liked the big horse barn, and always knew all of the horses by name and personality.

The first ones I remember—and always the most important ones—were Nickel and Dime, Dad's 15¢ team. They were brother and sister, a sorrel team Dad bought from Grandpa Griffith, who had raised them. Nick and Dime were never let out into the pasture, because the other horses fought them, and Dad was afraid of them being injured. I used to feel sorry for them and was glad to see them sometimes let out into the hog pasture for a little green grass. Always, the first thing they did was to lie down and roll, as if to scratch a long-tolerated itch. Dad curried and brushed them often to make up for not turning them out. When he needed to use a team, it was always Nick and Dime.

Dad's favorite team stood just inside the big east barn door, on the right. Across from them, in single stalls, were King and Queen. They were white horses and King always seemed older, quiet, and dignified. Somehow he always reminded me of Grandpa Ackley. When Queen died, her place was taken by Florrie, who was a dapple gray, with no personality that I can remember. After Florrie, that single stall was occupied by Sally, a small white horse that was Grandpa's favorite and the one he always drove on the buggy. We had two single-seat buggies—probably the second one was bought for Dad and Uncle Carl to drive to high school in Bryant.

When Grandpa went to a Farmers Elevator meeting in Erwin, he drove Sally, and if he fell asleep on the way home it didn't matter—Sally knew the way home.

Sally had one habit that captured our affection more than the other horses: when she was unhitched from the buggy or from a team from the field, or even if she had been in the pasture all day, she would take a drink of water from the horse-trough and then walk all the way around the barn, counter-clockwise, before going in to her stall. Sometimes she made two circuits. We always watched her do this, and we laughingly called her Sally-Walk-Around-the-Barn, which sounded like an Indian name. Dad tried opening the west barn door to see if she would go in that side, but she always walked all the way around to the east door.

Another of the old teams was Major and Nell, who always shared a stall. It is interesting to note that often the best teams were a male and female. When Nell died, Major was paired with Dan, a chestnut.

Dan caused quite a sensation one summer morning. I think we girls were hanging clothes on the line when we heard a commotion on the other side of the barn. We ran to see what it was, and found Dan thrashing around in one of the water troughs, his hindquarters wedged under one of the crosspieces. No one would have thought a horse could get himself stuck as he did under any circumstances, but there he was, frightened and angry, with the other horses agitated around him. We had to get the men from the field to help him out and it was a wonder that he had not broken a leg. He was scratched and bruised but soon recovered. We guessed that he had been chased and picked on by the other horses.

The last horses that were added to the teams, before the men bought the first tractor, belonged to Uncle Bliss. He agreed to accept horses as part repayment for the loss of his savings when the banks closed in 1932. The bank had foreclosed on the horses from someone else, and right at that time the farm needed horses. He got Barney and Jack, who made a team, and a pair of black horses named Dick and Dolly.

Barney was a large horse, sorrel color, with a Roman nose and the disposition of a bully. Jack was a timid bay. Since the black mare, Dolly, was young, Uncle Bliss decided to have her bred, and over a period of three or four years she produced three black colts—Prince, Little Dick, and Lady. It was interesting to have the pretty colts on the farm, but we didn't enjoy them very much. Dolly was short-tempered and snappy and not too bright. She showed her teeth often around the others. Her colts were much like her, and Uncle Bliss didn't have any patience with them. He yelled at them whenever he was around them, which didn't help their dispositions. We girls kept out of reach of their hooves and teeth whenever they were in the barn.

When I was little, I used to like to go with Dad to the barn in the dim light of late afternoon to feed the horses. I would climb up the ladder to the haymow with him and help him put hay down through the hole in the floor, and then carry pans of oats to put in each horse's feed box beside the manger that held hay. The barn was a few degrees warmer than the outside air—warmed by the 12 or 14 horses which stood facing each other across the central alleyway. It always seemed safe and friendly, with the sound of the horses munching hay and oats and occasionally stamping their feet.

But Dad was reluctant to allow us girls to really be around the horses and cattle very much. We were not expected to learn to milk cows or drive teams of horses in the field. None of us learned to hitch up a team, or to properly drive horses. We were shielded from matings and births, and were not encouraged to make pets of the animals. The men didn't want us around the barn when the vet came to "cut" the young pigs or calves, or when any animal was sick.

When Dad and Uncle Bliss had been working in the fields with teams of two to six horses, they watered the horses at noon and stabled them for an hour's rest. They usually worked in the afternoon until 6 o'clock. The horses were used to being stopped by the barn to have their harnesses unhooked from each other, as the traces were fastened to the harness on top of their rumps and the lines rolled up and fastened at the shoulder. They knew as soon as they were loosed, and would head for the water tank for a long drink. As each one finished, he or she would turn around and go to the proper stall in the barn to wait there until the harness was taken off and hung on a peg at the back of the stall. There was no fighting then—they were tired and hungry. As soon as bit and bridle were removed and the horse haltered and tied to the manger, he would turn his full attention to the mangerful of hay and the half-gallon or so of oats, with sometimes a little corn also in the feed box.

In summer the horses wore fly nets over their harnesses. These nets were a sort of blanket made of strings fastened to tapes. They moved with the horse, the fringe around the bottom swung back and forth, and the whole helped to keep away the flies that could make them miserable in hot weather.

(I read recently that Mary Ingalls, of the Little House books, learned to weave fly nets along with knitting and crocheting and playing the organ, in a college for the blind in Vinton, Iowa.)

The soft noses and lips of the horses were especially bothered by flies, and to give them some protection, someone had devised baskets made of wire screening, which covered the nose and mouth and fastened to the bridle. Our horses had fly nets and nose baskets for the fly season, but they always seemed glad to get the nose baskets off at night and to plunge their noses into the cool water tank.

The six or eight milk cows we had, along with the chickens, provided us with grocery money each week. We "traded" the eggs at the store for food we didn't raise and added the money from the cream check.

Dad and Uncle Bliss raised young cattle to sell as fat cattle to the meat packing plants. The early spring calves were turned out into the hog pen as soon as the weather was warm, and were fed hay to supplement pasture grass. I think they had access to ground grain all summer, too. After the corn was packed in the fall, they shared a daily feeding of ear corn with the pigs. Cattle and pigs were both efficient consumers of corn on the cob. Pigs bit off the kernels much as people do, but a good-sized steer or cow would take a whole ear of corn in its mouth and chew off the kernels. The cobs were cleaned of kernels either way.

One way we girls earned extra spending money in the summer was to pick up the dried corn cobs from the last fall into bushel baskets and then empty the baskets into an empty wagon Dad had placed in the pigpen for that purpose. We were paid a penny a basket! That almost seems like slave labor now, but a dollar would buy more than it does now. I was not afraid of the pigs when I was picking up cobs, for as soon as they knew I didn't have feed, they ignored me. The wagonload of cobs would be hauled in and shoveled into an empty bin to be dry kindling for starting winter fires.

Most of the cows were not milked but were kept to produce calves to raise for sale. What a din there was when these calves were separated from their mothers! When they were put in the hog pasture, with their mothers just across the fence but unreachable, it took several days for them to accept the inevitable.

Once in a while we had an unpredictable bull in the pasture, but mostly we weren't afraid of the cattle. We kids (including our Uncle Elwood Griffith and, a summer or two, cousins Leslie and Everett Ackley) trapped gophers in the pasture or climbed to the top of the hill just to enjoy the wide view and pick a few wildflowers—cowslips, cone flowers, violets.

Cattle are curious and would gather round any quiet activity such as setting gopher traps; they would stand in a quarter circle and stare fixedly at us. Sometimes this was a little frightening, but if we didn't make any threatening moves, they were quiet. If we suddenly rushed at them, or made threatening moves, they turned tail and galloped away in a bunch.

If it was a good year for grass, Dad and Uncle Bliss usually put most of the cattle, except the milk cows, into the pasture across the railroad track by the tree claim for the summer. There they had a new supply of grass and could go into the trees for shade when it was hot. Water was a problem, however.

Dad had had a shallow well, about 40–45 feet deep, dug near the north end of the pasture. I remember the discussion about where they would be most likely to find water, and something about a man who was a "dowser". But I don't remember whether they actually found a dowser to help.

Every day when there were cattle in that pasture, somebody had to go there to pump enough water to fill the metal tank. Usually the men did it, because it was a strenuous job for us. If the water in the tank was low, the cattle often came for a drink while it was being filled, and that made the job an even harder one! A block of salt stood near the water tank—sometimes we used to help ourselves to a chip while we were there. The entire block was always licked away by the end of the summer.

In winter, the cattle were kept in the home pasture. They always had access to shelter in a shed attached to the old barn, and its manger was filled with hay. They were also fed corn fodder from a long stack beside the feed lot.

In 1927, all the calves died.

Every winter, the weaned calves were kept in a pen in the old barn and fed skim milk and grain and hay until the weather warmed up and they could be put into the pasture with the pigs.

That summer, before they could be turned out, they got sick. One died, and then another and another, and the veterinarian could do nothing to stop the disease from spreading. Dr. Truman called it "hemorrhagic septicemia", and I can remember saying it over and over, fascinated by the sound of the big words. I was nine years old at the time, and I was driven by a fascination I could not control to watch the operation of hitching a reluctant team of horses to the carcass of a dead calf, pulling it out of the barn, pulling it around the corner of the barn to where another "grave" had been dug. A farm road ran alongside the feed lot behind the barn, and corn fodder was always stacked beside it for winter feeding. In a couple of weeks time, as more calves died, a cemetery had been made there, and the pen in the barn was empty.

The pen was left empty for more than a year, and well cleaned before more calves were put into it. The dread disease did not reappear. I had a child's horror of the area because it was a place of death, and I didn't go near it for a long time.

The farm had no electricity before 1945 or '46, so there was no refrigeration. That made a difference in the way we stored food, especially meat. Early in the spring every year, probably in March when the weather was still cool, Dad planned for butchering pigs for the main part of our summer meat supply. He would fatten four or five chosen pigs, because we needed the lard. We didn't know about cholesterol then, and lard was used for cooking and baking, for making soap, and for preserving meat.

Preparation for butchering time nudged the whole family out of the lethargy of winter. All of the stone jars and crocks were washed and readied, the sausage and lard press was brought up from the cellar, the salt mixture for preserving hams and bacon was bought. Knives were sharpened, and the twenty- and thirty-gallon stone jars in the cellar were cleaned.

On the day of the butchering, Dad would get out the large iron kettle which held thirty or forty gallons of water, hang it on a heavy pole between two strong supports, fill it with water, and build a fire underneath. He would shoot the pigs and then bleed them immediately. Then they were dunked in the boiling water.

The men had to be careful that they didn't scald the pigs too long, which would cook the skin, but just long enough so that the bristles would be loosened and could be easily scraped off. After boiling, they were laid on a makeshift platform, and the bristles were scraped off with a knife or a special scraping tool that looked something like a biscuit cutter. When the scraping was finished, they were hung up and the entrails removed. They were usually hung overnight to cool out—to remove all body heat.

The next day the work began for Mom, and Grandma while she lived at the farm. After Grandma moved to town, she sometimes came out for a day to help with big jobs. A neighbor or two often came to help butcher, too, in anticipation of being given some fresh liver to take home that day, and the promise of a good roast or some spare ribs a day or so later.

Dad did the actual cutting up of the different parts, putting the scraps from trimming the hams into a tub to be ground into sausage. Mom cut up the fat which was slowly cooked— "tried out", as it was called—in kettles on the kitchen stove for lard. It had to be thoroughly cooked, but not overcooked, pure and white when cool. Lard was separated from the cracklings in the lard press. The lard press forced the hot grease out through a spout at the bottom, and pressed the cracklings into a solid cake.

The chickens liked the cracklings. And we always kept back a little for cracklin' corn bread, or even cracklin' cookies.

Lard was stored in five- and ten-gallon jars with wooden covers in the cellar. It would keep quite well on the cool cellar floor until butchering time the following year. If, by chance, any of it should become rancid, it could always be made into soap.

We all helped grind the sausage, but Dad seasoned it, mixing it with his hands in a clean wash tub. We always watched for the time when he decided that it was probably seasoned just right and would fry up a sample for us to taste.

Sausage was preserved in several ways. Some of it was packed into half-gallon crocks and baked in the oven like a meatloaf, then covered with hot lard. When these cooled, they were stored in the cellar the same as lard, and would keep for a few months.

Some sausage was put into casings, which were then tied into rings and smoked. Since these sausages were not cooked, they were usually canned in quart jars. Sausage casings were the small intestines of the pigs, cleaned and washed, then soaked in salt water, scraped, then soaked again. I can remember Mother cleaning the strips by drawing them across a small wooden tool, shaped something like a crochet hook, which she whittled when she needed one.

Pork chops and spare ribs were not so plentiful and some were eaten fresh. If the weather was too warm, and we couldn't keep the meat frozen for a while, Mother would fry or bake them, pack them in stone jars, and pour hot lard over them to preserve them for two or three months.

I always hated to be sent down to the cellar to get enough pork chops for dinner, because I had to feel around in the cool lard with my fingers to find them.

The hams and bacon were Dad's job. He preferred a dry cure—a mixture of salt, brown sugar, saltpeter, and spices, rubbed into the meat from all sides. The hams and bacon were then placed in the large stone jars. The salt mixture dried out the meat and penetrated through it over a few weeks time. Every few days the pieces were taken out, and more of the cure was rubbed in. I can't remember just how long this curing process lasted, but it seems as though it was a month or six weeks.

After the meat was judged sufficiently cured, it was hung in the smoke house over a slow-burning smoky fire of sawdust. The process of smoking the meat lasted until the weather began to be warm in the spring. The meat was now sufficiently cured so that it needed no refrigeration and would probably keep for years, since it was heavily salted and dried. Each piece was then put into a muslin bag and wrapped in heavy brown paper and hung in the cellarway over the stairs. They would keep well into the fall and following winter. When we cooked ham or bacon, we always "freshened" it by putting it on the stove in cold water, bringing it to a boil, and pouring off the water, sometimes twice, before it was fried. When most of the meat was sliced off, the ham bone was boiled with potatoes and carrots and cabbage, and we always looked forward to that boiled dinner.

Meat cured in this way provided farm families with a source of summer protein. Many barrels of it traveled across the country with wagon trains. I was glad when modern refrigeration made locker plants available for storing large amounts of frozen meat—I liked "store-bought" ham and bacon much better!

One other kind of sausage we liked was "head cheese", made actually from the animals' heads, which were cooked in the wash boiler. Then bits of meat were cut up in pieces, seasoned, and allowed to cool in some of the broth they were cooked in. This would congeal like gelatin and mold the whole into a loaf which could be sliced easily.

Besides the fresh pork liver, we ate the brains, and considered them a rare delicacy—but we learned not to talk about eating them to most of our friends, who didn't appreciate the idea.

I really didn't have to help very much with the cutting-up and curing of meat, because by the time I was old enough to be helpful, Dad had begun taking the pigs to the butcher in town, who did all of the work, even to the curing of ham and bacon. The butcher would wrap all of the pieces and put the packages into the locker we rented in his freezer. He didn't make sausage like Dad, though, or head cheese like Mom's.

8

Household and Garden

Spring housecleaning was always done about the first week of June, right after school was out for the summer. We spent a strenuous week "turning" out the house from top to bottom. Housecleaning usually started with the bedrooms upstairs, where a ladder was needed to take off the storm windows. After that we scrubbed floors and washed windows, curtains, and blankets. We slept in flannel sheets all winter, but in the spring these were put away and the muslin and percale were brought out.

Uncle Bliss's mattress had to be taken outdoors and beaten with a carpet beater. He slept in his underwear, which he changed only once or twice a week, and his mattress was filled with the dust of the fields. We would beat it awhile, then sweep off the dust that came to the surface, and repeat the process.

Rugs that could not be washed had to be beaten the same way, for there was no electricity to run a vacuum cleaner.

Downstairs, one of the first jobs to be done was to move the heating stoves out of the living room and dining room and store them on the front porch for the summer. While Grandpa still lived on the farm, the parlor heater was a large upright hard coal stove, resplendent with chrome, and with isinglass windows on three sides. I remember the warm glow of the coal fire through those small window on a cold night. The dining room stove was a small wood-burning heater.

As spring cleaning continued, the walls were brushed or washed or painted, the windows washed, and the dust accumulation of the winter was brushed out of the windowsills. The lace curtains were taken down, washed, stiffly starched with boiled starch, and stretched on wooden frames made especially for that purpose. These frames were lengths of light lumber with strips of muslin or ticking tacked along their length. The frames were laid out to the size needed and fastened together with C-clamps; then the starched curtains were pinned, one on top of the other, to the cloth strips, and the whole thing set outside in the breeze to dry.

The green roller shades were cleaned and mended; usually, the slot for the bottom stick had rotted and torn, and the shade had to be trimmed, then a new slot stitched for a new stick.

We cleaned drawers and polished furniture and waxed floors. The linoleum floors were given a good scrubbing and then polished with paste wax. After the wax had dried, the floor had to be polished with a weighted lamb's wool pad on a handle, or—what was more fun—by a couple of girls sliding back and forth across it in old socks!

By the end of the week we were tired and satisfied, and the house smelled like starched curtains and floor wax and furniture polish—and we were pleased with it.

The farm kitchen was small and always seemed crowded. One wall accommodated the door to the dining room and a large Monarch cast iron cook stove, called a "range". The old kitchen range was cumbersome and it took a lot of work to keep it clean. We burned wood and corn cobs in it, and these had to be carried in—and the ashes out again. The five-gallon hot water reservoir always seemed to be in need of a few pails of water from the cistern, and every afternoon the ash pan had to be carried out and emptied.

On the south wall was the woodbox, with hooks above it for hanging wet jackets and caps. Wet mittens were put to dry in the "warming oven" above the cooking surface. The door to the cellar stairs was beside the wood box, and beside it, but on the east wall, was the outside door. On the back of this door a roller towel always hung, so that it would be handy to the white porcelain sink that stood on an iron stand. Underneath, a five-gallon slop pail held the waste water and kitchen garbage. A cabinet under the east window held pots and pans, and its surface was where we peeled potatoes and prepared food. A water pail with a dipper always stood here, and we all drank from it.

One of the summer jobs we girls all hated was washing the cream separator. We washed dishes after every meal—never were they allowed to wait till the next one—and the separator had to be washed after the morning milking and breakfast.

The big milk tank which sat on the top of the separator was heavy and awkward, and the strainer was messy, its cotton pad filled with dust from the cows. The milk and cream spouts were awkward and had to be cleaned with a long-handled brush. But the worst part of all were the "cups". These were more like nested funnels, which fitted rather snugly over a heavy center post on a base.

Those 18 or 20 cups first had to be taken off the center post, threaded by holes in the sides onto a large holder that was something like a giant safety-pin, and then separated and scrubbed, one by one, with a stiff brush. After this, they were rinsed with boiling water and hung to dry. Even though the milk was strained through a felt pad, there was always fine dust which had not been caught, and in the summer the residue soured overnight. It was a job we learned to finish as soon as possible, to get it out of the way.

Since we had no refrigeration, we sold sour cream to the creamery in Bryant, and later, to the one in Lake Norden, which sent a truck around on a regular route to collect a can of cream and leave a sterilized can in its place. We drank skim milk, and in summer it would stay sweet until noon on the cool cellar floor. Skim milk was also fed to calves and cats, and even to the pigs. Mom made good cottage cheese from it, which she sold to one of the stores in Bryant.

We used sour cream to make a salad dressing for lettuce, and to make creamed vegetables or potatoes. We girls liked it on bread, too, sprinkled with salt and pepper, in place of butter.

I remember the sound of the cream separator. It was hard to turn, and we were never allowed to do it. When the men started it, it turned slowly, and a heavy metal ball on a short arm on the handle would click twice with every rotation of the handle. When the turner reached the correct speed for separating the cream from the milk, the ball was silent—everything was turning fast enough.

When the old garden area was worn out, Mother decided to move the garden to the north side of the driveway where there had been grass for many years. Here she had plenty of room for a couple of rows of early potatoes and some early sweet corn, and the Hubbard squash which sprawled over a lot of space. She planted a new asparagus bed and a strawberry bed, and set out raspberry bushes.

Dad would plow the garden in the spring, first giving it a good application of rotted manure. Fertility was not the problem—it was water that we often lacked. When we set out plants of tomatoes or cabbage, we had to carry pails of water from the well near the barn. We could have used a tank of water beside the garden. I have often wondered why we didn't do a number of things that would have made life easier.

After eating mostly canned vegetables all winter, except for potatoes and carrots and maybe a few parsnips, we looked forward to the fresh ones from the garden. The first green things in the garden in the spring were always the winter onions. I thought they were too strong, but the men liked them and Mom used them in cooking. Soon there was asparagus, and we could never get enough of that. The asparagus that I buy in markets now seems tasteless compared to what I remember. Maybe it's because I don't make creamed asparagus with thick cream the way we used to have it!

When I was small, we had a cabbage barrel set into the ground in the garden near the house. It would be cleaned out and filled with mature cabbages wrapped in newspaper. These were covered with a mound of straw, a wooden cover, and more straw. Cabbages stored this way usually kept fresh until well into the winter.

Mom raised all of the common vegetables in the garden besides the potatoes, and if it was a good year, not too wet and cool, we were pleased to have new potatoes and creamed new peas for the Fourth of July. Gourmet food! We learned to look forward to and enjoy every vegetable in its season.

Summer was always the time for canning vegetables and fruit. All of us who were old enough to shell peas or snap beans or shuck sweet corn, even any visiting cousins, would be expected to help. Mom would go out to the garden right after breakfast was over, leaving us to wash the dishes, separator and milk pails, and to tidy the house. When she came from the garden with pails full of peas or beans, we all sat outside in a shady place and shelled or snapped until they were ready to process. Those were pleasant times, and we all sat on boxes or stools, with pans in our laps, and visited, or listened to Mom tell of her childhood, or gossiped, and felt good about sharing a needed job.

In the first years that I can remember, we canned vegetables, fruit, and even meat, in a hot water bath canner on the kerosene stove in the pantry, or in a steamer with racks on two levels above a water pan in the bottom. Nowadays no one would feel that canning meat or peas or corn this way would be safe, but I cannot recall that many jars of vegetables spoiled, and if one did, it was noticeable right away. Mom always boiled or steamed whatever she was canning as much as an hour longer than the directions called for, and felt they were safe. We were well aware that this method was not the safest way, and Mom soon invested in a large pressure canner. This held only about six quarts at a time, but it was much faster and safer. Whenever we added some jars of vegetables or meat to the shelves in the basement, we couldn't help but stand and admire them for a few minutes.

The dry, cold winds of winter were hard on fruit trees, and most people didn't try very hard to have an orchard. We bought peaches, plums, cherries, pears, and strawberries by the crate and canned them for winter pies and sauce. One neighbor tried raising strawberries and for a few years had so many that they let people come in and pick their own at reasonable prices. We bought grapes for jelly and jam, and some years there was a good crop of chokecherries at nearby Cherry Lake. We would go in the car and spend an afternoon picking them. I didn't much like chokecherry jam, but the jelly was delicious.

We liked corn, but we didn't eat the young ears of field corn as many people did. Dad always planted several rows of Golden Bantam sweet corn in one of the fields, along with enough potatoes to fill the bin in the basement. The potatoes would last until the new crop was mature enough so that we could dig a pailful at a time in the summer. I remember digging new potatoes during one of the dry years, when I had to dig up many hills to fill the pail, and the ones I dug were mostly the size of large marbles. We ate those boiled with the skins on, or put them through a potato ricer to get rid of the skins.

Sweet corn was best fresh from the field, and we would pick it just before our noon dinnertime. When we were canning corn, we would go to the field with the car and fill sacks with corn, but only so much as we could take back and process quickly. It had to be shucked, the silks cleaned off, and then the kernels cut off the cobs and blanched. The kernels were blanched by putting them first into boiling water and then into the coldest water we had. Then they were packed into jars, the jars filled with boiling water, and salt added. When ready, the jars were processed in the pressure canner. Before we got that new canner, they were processed in boiling water, or in the steam canner for four hours.

One year Dad decided to raise his own soup beans. He planted a couple of long rows with the corn planter, but we had to harvest the dry bean plants by hand. The worst part was threshing them—the dry, brittle plants were piled on a canvas and beaten with a carpet beater. After that, we learned first-hand what winnowing was all about. On a windy day we tossed them into the air for the wind to blow away the broken pods and stems. It was more work than it was worth, and after that experience we bought dry beans.

In the last 40 years, I have often seen replicas of Mother's old wooden washing machine in museums—but hers was not run by woman-power. Mom had a small gasoline engine outside the back entry where the machine stood, connected to the washing machine inside by two belts and a pulley.

Wash day began on Sunday evening, when the big copper wash boiler was set on the kitchen range and filled with water. The water was carried pailful by pailful, from the cistern outside.

The cistern pump, at least, was a great improvement over drawing water up with a rope and pail. The family had had the latest improvement in cistern pumps installed when I was small, partly as a safety measure. It never needed to be primed, and made filling a pail by turning a crank a luxury when compared to drawing it up with a rope.

On Monday morning, when the water was hot, Mom would shave a bar or two of homemade lye soap and put it into the wash boiler. When the soap was dissolved in the hot water, white clothes and linens were usually boiled in it before the water was dipped out into pails and put into the wooden tub of the washing machine. Two tubs full of cold water stood beside the wash machine, with a hand-turned wringer fastened between them. One usually was colored with bluing, which helped to whiten the linens. Mother had already made a pan of thick starch by pouring boiling water over dry corn starch mixed with water, and this mixture was then diluted to the proper consistency to stiffen the linens, or just to add a light finish to cotton dresses and shirts.

I usually enjoyed hanging clothes on the wire lines which stretched between the smoke house and the privy, and beyond that to a stout post by the woodpile. In summer the clothes dried quickly in the wind. While they flapped on the line, we emptied the wash machine, scrubbed the shed floor, and used a pailful of the warm soapy water to scrub out the privy with a broom. I always took great satisfaction in destroying spider webs and sending the spiders scurrying for corners.

Wash day was always a busy one, and we couldn't forget that it would soon be noon, when the men would come in hungry for a substantial meal.

Sometimes we needed to do other things as well as wash clothes on Monday, and it was always a matter of great pride to be able to say that we had "washed and ironed and baked bread", all on Monday!

For many years we ironed clothes with a set of sad irons (I don't know why they were called "sad") which were heated on the stove, and clamped into a holder with a wooden handle. Usually three were used, two of them heating on the stove all the time. Mom finally bought—with chicken money—a gas iron that was heated by a small gas tank attached behind the hand grip of the iron. This was an improvement in some ways, but it was heavy and cumbersome, and hot to hold. We told ourselves we liked it better and continued to use it.

Grandpa and Grandma didn't buy an electric washing machine when they moved to town. I don't think Grandpa was ever very comfortable with electricity. One time, when I had finished ironing for Grandma in their kitchen, I simply disconnected the iron cord from the overhead cord which was the only outlet in the kitchen. Grandpa was nearby, and he insisted that I also turn the wall switch to off, so that electricity that we weren't using would not be wasted as it escaped from the end of the cord (which now had no bulb attached and no cord plugged into it). In vain I argued that it was already off, but he would not listen. In my 15-year-old assurance that I knew how it worked, I am sure I irritated him to the point where he could not give in, even had he been persuaded that I was right. I knew he had a good understanding of things mathematical, and could not see why he couldn't understand this!

Whatever the reason, my grandparents washed clothes with a kind of pounder that was like an upside-down funnel attached to a stout handle like a broomstick. Grandpa did the heavy work of lifting pails of hot water from the wash boiler on the kerosene stove, and he wielded the "washer" in the tub of hot, soapy water. It made a nice business-like sucking sound and seemed to get the clothes clean.

One day the Watkins Man came around selling his usual line of spices and flavorings. Mom usually bought vanilla from him, and sometimes a bottle of concentrated fruit flavoring called Nectar, which we used to make summer drinks, like the Kool-Aid of the present day. That day, he showed us a gadget that caught my eye. It was a device for showering, consisting of a spigot that could be screwed into a hole made in the side of a milk pail, near the bottom, to which was attached a short hose that ended in a head like a shower or sprinkling can. It looked like a good idea to Mom and me, and she bought one.

When my Dad saw it, he said, "Where are you going to use it?" and we had to think about that awhile. We soon came up with the idea of turning the old smokehouse into a summer shower house. It wasn't used for smoking meat any more, and stood empty.

Dad soon became interested in the project and agreed that we could put a cement floor in the smoke house, which he and I did. We even made a drain channel that directed the water out under the back wall and into the pigpen. Dad made a slatted wood platform to stand on, and we were in business.

Most days were hot and sunny enough to warm two or three pails of water, set on the back steps, to a comfortable temperature for a shower, and Dad soon made a habit of enjoying one in the evening after a day's work in the field. Although Mom had gone along with the project, we could never persuade her to use it. She preferred taking her baths in the house. Uncle Bliss didn't think much of it, either. We girls and Dad were the ones who appreciated it.

Before we had the shower house, and even with it in use, Mom would see that we washed our feet if we had been working outside. We were never allowed to go barefoot because we found too many nails around the buildings, and the dooryard was stony. Tetanus, or lockjaw, was feared, and it was common knowledge that injuries around a barnyard were especially dangerous.

I remember sitting on the cement steps by the back door at dusk after a hot, windy day, with a pan of warm water, soap, and a towel, and easing my tired, dusty feet. The hot, relentless wind of the day had softened to a caressing breeze that dried my feet and took away the weariness of the day.

I think these were the times when our family felt a closeness that no one had the time nor the inclination for during the desperate years of the drought. We would sit and talk, and the worries about whether we could keep going would be eased for a little while.

9

The Rolling of the Year

When the first warm days of spring began to melt the snow, the pulse of farm life quickened. No longer were the activities house-bound. Dad and Uncle Bliss found things to do outside instead of napping or reading in the afternoons. Dad always looked over the machinery in the spring and made repairs. Mom ordered garden seeds from Gurney's Seed and Nursery at Yankton, or from Henry Field's in Shenandoah, Iowa.

Dad spent some afternoons preparing seed corn for planting (this was before the days of hybrid corn). He took the ears of corn off the drying racks in the haymow and shelled them in the hand-turned sheller. He always chose the best ears of corn in the fall to save for seed. He took those to the haymow where he shucked them and impaled them on sharp metal spikes that held two ears pointing in opposite directions. Between the two ears, an upside-down V in the spike fitted over the circular iron bands of the drying rack. These racks looked like stacks of rings, about four feet in diameter and five feet high.

A full rack of the yellow ears was beautiful, and it lifted one's spirits just to see it on a gloomy winter day. The bottom row was a foot or so off the floor, and I could lie on my back and wiggle my head underneath, and look up at the golden "silo" on the inside. I used to be happy to help Dad shuck the corn to find the best ears, because sometimes we would find a completely red ear, and that was always mine. Dad never planted red corn, but a few red ears always appeared, and I always wondered where they came from.

The best potatoes were sorted out from the bin in the cellar and put aside to be cut up and planted. Mom and Dad always planted a couple of rows in the garden at the time it was plowed, dropping the pieces into the open furrow, to be covered by the next furrow as the plow made another round.

Seed wheat, oats, barley, and rye were always cleaned in the spring. The "fanning mill" that did the job was lowered by ropes and pulleys from its place in the rafters of the granary, and all of the seed grain run through it. The mill consisted mostly of slanting horizontal sieves that were shaken to sort out small weed seeds and other unwanteds. The small gasoline engine that usually powered the washing machine was hitched to the fanning mill, which was noisy and dusty.

The other grain cleaner was used especially for oats. It was like a section of road culvert lined with heavy flannel and mounted horizontally on a slant. The oats were fed into the upper end, and, as the cylinder turned, the black, bearded kernels of wild oats caught on the flannel—most of them, at least—and the smoother "tame" oats rolled out at the bottom. The little engine powered this, too.

This was also the time for cleaning out the cattle shed and spreading the rotted manure on the fields. When farming people first began to settle in the prairie states—Indiana, Illinois, and on west—they questioned the fertility of the land where no trees grew. It was only when they began to plow the grasslands and raise crops that they realized the depth and fertility of the prairie land. Commercial fertilizers were rarely used and not very available in those days. Not until the prairie states had been farmed for some years, and the droughts and winds of the 1930s had stripped off much topsoil, did there come to be a market for commercial fertilizer.

In Summertime, the livin' wasn't easy. For the men, summer meant long days in the field, coming home tired, hot, and dusty with a team of tired horses, which had to be unharnessed and fed. There was the milking still to be done, and probably pigs to feed, too. We usually raised about 40 or 50 head of hogs to be sold in the fall every year.

After school was out in the spring, it usually fell to us girls to do the evening "chores", as soon as we were able to handle a pitchfork and carry a pail of feed.

The horse chores were a trial, because we had to push hay down through the open hole in the haymow floor to feed 12 or 14 horses. Although the hay looked soft and light, it settled over the winter into a firm stack, and we had to wrestle every forkful from it. After we had pushed a good amount through the hatch, we climbed down the ladder and carried it with the pitchfork to fill the mangers for all the horses. At one end of the barn was an oats bin, and from there, we put one or two panfuls of oats into each horse's own feed box. If that particular horse wasn't working long days in the field, it would get only one panful, or none.

I really hated feeding the pigs. By the time the summer weather was hot, the young ones were weaned from their mothers and were always ravenous for the mash that they were fed every evening. Dad or Uncle Bliss usually mixed a 50-gallon drum of ground barley, corn, and feed supplements with water early in the day. An afternoon in the hot sun caused a mild fermentation, and by evening it had a strong, sour smell. Whoever fed the pigs had to fill buckets with this mash, lift them over a section of wooden fence, and empty them into the wooden troughs in the pigpen.

The pigs always frightened me a little when I had to feed them. They crowded and jostled each other around my legs and around the trough, and I was always afraid I would fall down in the midst of them. Pigs will happily eat meat, and I have known Dad to dispose of a dead horse by dragging the carcass into the pigpen. In a couple of days only the biggest bones were left.

As soon as the corn was picked in the fall, a wagonload of ears of corn was pulled into the pigpen, and some fed to the pigs every day. They cleaned the kernels off the cobs without wasting one, and for a while, as they ate, there was a mighty sound of chomping.

Mom usually took care of feeding the chickens, but we often helped her carry pails of water for them. I always enjoyed gathering eggs in the summer, because there were many places to look besides the chicken house. The hens would hide nests in both barns, and there were many good corners that were hard to find. Sometimes one would choose a sheltered place under a piece of machinery outside, and we wouldn't find her nest until she came clucking into the yard followed by eight or ten fluffy chicks. If we saw a hen come proudly cackling from any place except the hen house, we searched for a nest.

We girls never learned to milk cows because Dad didn't really think it right for women to have to do farmwork, and didn't insist on us learning to harness and drive horses. Mom had learned to milk cows when she was a girl, and she helped out at harvest time, but our cows weren't used to women and were skittish.

We girls didn't often have to clean out the manure from the stalls, either. The men usually left that job for a rainy day; then they would pull the manure spreader into the alleyway of the barn and work inside.

I think Uncle Bliss would have preferred that Mom and Dad have boys instead of girls, and he often made admiring references to a neighbor family with four daughters, all of whom could harness and drive a six-horse team and do field work.

We always looked forward to harvest time—everybody worked extra hard, but the routine changed, and we had the sense of all working together to achieve an important goal.

For many years, the grain was cut with two horse-drawn binders; we cut the grain, gathered it into bundles, tied each bundle with twine, and held them until several were ready to be dumped into a pile on the grain stubble. Next, it had to be shocked, and there was no machine to do that. We girls did our share, although we were only required to shock grain if it urgently needed to be gotten up off the ground when rain threatened. We usually shocked oats, which was the lighter in weight, although I remember at least once struggling with rye bundles which were as tall as I was. You started with a bundle in each hand, and you set them down together, forcefully, so that the upstanding stubble would hold them up. Then you set other bundles around them until you had ten or a dozen, depending on the size, with the heads of the grain massed compactly together at the top so that rain would quickly run off. Sometimes shocks were "capped" with one more bundle, to protect the heads.

When we were cutting and shocking grain, it was always a welcome break in the afternoon to stop for lunch—usually a peanut butter and jelly sandwich and a cookie and a cool drink. Since we didn't have any kind of refrigeration, we could not take a chance on a meat or egg sandwich spoiling on a hot day. Sometimes Mom came out to the field in the old car to bring us a sandwich and a jug of lemonade cooled with well water.

We didn't have a thermos jug then, and we took water to the field in a stoneware jug which had been wrapped in burlap tied tight around it, and then dunked in the water tank. The evaporation of the water kept the contents of the jug reasonably cool. We also had canvas water bags, kept cool by the evaporation of the water that leaked out slowly.

Just before World War II, Dad and Uncle Bliss bought their first tractor, a green John Deere with metal wheels and no rubber tires. Dad converted the old binders from horse-drawn to tractor-pulled machines by shortening the tongues and putting on the proper hitch, and that was what we used as long as I helped out at harvest time. I soon learned to drive the tractor, and I liked that much better than having to shock grain! It was not until after the war that they began to hire a combine to harvest grain, and that did away with so much of the back-breaking labor of the harvest.

The threshing was usually done in August by a man who owned a separator and the engine to run it. Six or eight neighbors, working together, formed a "thresh run", with each helping the others. The earliest threshing rigs that I remember were powered by a steam engine, which required a team of four men to operate. One man ran the steam engine, and one was the separator man, whose job it was to see that the bundles went smoothly into that machine and that the straw blower was moved regularly to make a good stack. He usually carried an oil can as he climbed over the rattling machine. Two more were required to haul coal and water to feed the chuffing steam engine. In later years, gas fired the engine instead of coal. For some reason the man who drove the old truck with the water tank was called the "water monkey". We usually threshed grain in the pasture, because the straw stack provided a little feed and some protection for the cattle in winter. They would browse for the spilled grain and gradually eat a tunnel into the stack.

I think that when the family first came to South Dakota, the men hauled the bundles of grain from the fields and stacked them near the barns so that the grain could be left until later in the fall to be threshed. The separator would then be pulled between the stacks, and a team of only two or three men were needed to pitch the grain bundles onto the conveyer belt.

When my memory begins, however, the grain shocks were left in the field, to be hauled in to the separator in haywagons (at threshing time, they were called "bundle wagons"). It took about six bundle wagons to supply the separator. Sometimes they had an extra man, called a "spike pitcher" to help unload the wagons.

Dinner on those days was a big production, with the dining table stretched to its longest— all six extra leaves included. Every housewife tried to provide a good hearty meal, with pie for dessert. There would be roast beef or stewed chicken with noodles, mashed potatoes, vegetables, cabbage slaw, pickles, plenty of bread and butter and jam.

A bench outside the back door was supplied with two or three wash basins, soap, and clean roller towels, and also a couple of pails of water that were set out early in the morning to warm in the sun. The men washed the dust from their hands and faces and combed their hair in front of the mirror.

The machine men were usually the first to appear for dinner, because all of the others had to water and feed their horses. Dad and Uncle Bliss were usually last, having had to unload the last load of threshed grain. For this the elevator was set up beside the granary, the little gas engine which usually ran the wash machine was hooked up to it, and the endless chain of baffles started in motion to carry the grain to the top of the granary where it would be shunted into the bins.

We usually had the threshing machine at our place two days in a row, because our farm was larger than those around us; and then after everyone had had a turn, they would come back for another day or so to finish up. The men kept track of the number of days' work at every farm, and those who worked more time were paid for it.

On threshing days, we women would no sooner finish the stacks of dinner dishes than we would have to begin preparing lunch, which we took out to the machine at 3 p.m. We made sandwiches of leftover meat or the old standby, bologna, and took them, with cookies or a cake and the large old copper-bottomed coffee pot filled to the brim, which had a piece of cloth wedged into the open spout to keep the coffee from slopping out on the trip to the field. Coffee was started with cold water and ground coffee that had been mixed with a raw egg—shell and all. When it came to a boil, it was set off the heat and a dash of cold water added to settle the grounds and help clear it. I remember sitting in the passenger's seat of the old Chevy and holding the old coffee pot clear of the floor so that the hot liquid would not slop out onto me, while the car jounced over the rough track to the field.

The men enjoyed a break, and we all enjoyed visiting with them as they sat on the ground and ate and joked. The machinery didn't stop.

We had to feed only the machine men for supper, and they were happy with cold meat and leftovers. All the neighbors went home.

As I recall those busy harvest days, one of my strongest memories is of the sounds of threshing. Usually the mornings were clear and quiet and sounds could be heard a long way. I would go outside in the clear morning and hear the men coming with their teams and hayracks. The horses were fresh and frisky, and would begin to trot, the driver would call to them, whistle or sing, and the jingle of the harness, the rumble of the wagon wheels, all would be carried on the morning air. The steam engine and later the gasoline engine each had its own particular running sound, and the big separator, as soon as the belt was tightened and it was put in gear, rumbled and ground and rattled as it beat out the grain and blew out the straw and chaff. You had to shout to be heard near it.

The teams going home were tired, and the men, too, although sometimes one of the younger fellows, glad that another day was done, would whip up his team and go prancing out of the driveway with a flourish and a jangle of harness and rattle of wagon.

We girls had extra jobs during threshing time, because the men didn't get home until 6:30 or 7 o'clock. We did most of the chores, which meant struggling in the haymow to dig out enough packed hay to fill all of the horse mangers, and putting grain in the feed bins of those who were working. In my mind, feeding the pigs was the worst job of all, carrying pailfuls of the slightly fermented mash from the barrel that had stood in the hot sun all day, lifting them over the fence, and racing the 40-odd half-grown hungry pigs to the troughs to empty them. The first pailfuls were the worst, and I was really a little afraid of those chomping teeth that surrounded me.

Before I started to school, I used to ride to town in the fall with Dad, sitting high atop a triple-box wagon-load of grain to be sold at the elevator. I can remember that it was a grand feeling to be up so high on the spring seat, way above the horses' backs. It took a long time for the horses to walk the three-and-a-half miles to town with the heavy load of grain, and I expect that Dad liked the company.

I was fascinated by the mechanics of unloading the grain at the elevator. They first un-hitched the horses, fastened the front wagon wheels on a platform that tilted upwards, and then removed the end-gate from the lowest tier of "boxes" of the wagon. This let the grain pour out of the wagon into a pit underneath the platform, from where it was lifted by an elevator system into the high bins.

Dad often combined such a trip with a visit to the blacksmith shop, which was near the elevator, and we would watch while Fred Geisler sharpened a plowshare, or refitted a metal rim on a wagon wheel, or put new iron shoes on a horse. The shop was an interesting place, and I liked to watch as the smith pounded the first white-hot, then the red-hot metal, and then plunged it into a tank of water, where it made a great hissing sound with clouds of steam.

The wooden wagons that were used on farms in those days could be made shallow or deep as the need arose by the addition of more "boxes". The basic wagon was called a lumber wagon, but whether the name came from the fact that it was almost entirely made of wood, or that it had originally been used to haul lumber or logs, I don't know. However, it was a very versatile vehicle.

The sides and the ends of the "boxes" were in separate pieces—two sides and two ends which fitted together with grooves to make it one "box" high. It was often used this way to haul fence repairs and tools to various parts of the farm. If a larger capacity was needed, another box was added like the first and held in place by the braces on the sides, which slipped down over the box below. The end of any box could be removed without disturbing the sides, but I think that there was always one end which folded in the middle for easier removal, and that was the one used on the bottom tier of a load of grain.

Usually no more than three sections were added, making it a triple-box wagon. For corn picking by hand, however, a fourth side was added on the left (if the picker was right-handed). The picker could then toss each ear of corn at the bang board, and it would fall right into the wagon.

The wagon could also be stripped down to its floor and running gears, and used to haul loads of trimmed logs of wood from the tree claim. For this kind of load, they added four strong upright supports—two on each side—and piled the logs high between them, with the narrower ends hanging out behind.

The basic wagon, with a wooden rack instead of the stacked boxes, was a hayrack. One of these wagons always stood on the south side of the horse barn, ready for hay-making in the summer, threshing later on, and for hauling hay from stacks in the field or straw from the stack in the pasture in the winter.

These wagons were pulled by one team of horses, and had a long wooden tongue to which the horses were hitched—at the back by traces from their collars to the double trees, and at the front also by a chain to the collar. They pulled from their collars to the double trees—the front only held the tongue up. A tongue was not absolutely necessary, but was useful in keeping the horses evenly spaced and out of each other's way.

Banking the house for winter was one of the routine jobs in the fall. Dad would first cover the foundation and the lower part of the wood siding with builders' paper—I remember it was pink—which was fastened on with wood lath strips. Then, when the weather was freezing, he and Uncle Bliss would haul fresh manure mixed with straw from the horse barn and pile it against the paper, where it would freeze and form a barrier against cold drafts that blew from the northwest.

I can't remember how long this was kept up, but it was certainly until about the end of the 1920s. I can remember that I understood the need to try to keep the floors warmer, but I didn't much like the kind of weatherproofing they used. Eventually, plain earth was used instead of the manure (I think my mother had some input there) and finally just the heavy paper was all that was used. As soon as the drought was over and times were better, the living room and dining room stoves were discarded and a gas floor furnace was installed to heat both rooms.

When the weather got really cold, and the thermometer would register –25° or –30°, the old farmhouse was not really warm, even with three stoves. We had storm windows, but they didn't fit tight, and there was always a draft around them. There was no insulation in the walls or attic, and no caulking around the windows. The windows were often thick with frost in the mornings. I used to study the designs the frost made and see forests and starry skies and fairy landscapes in crystal tracings, and then Jack Frost seemed a real and very busy fairy.

On winter days when it was too cold for the men to do more than take care of the livestock, they would sit in the dining room with their feet on the fenders of the little heater and read or doze or listen to the radio. Uncle Bliss was fond of lying on the floor on a rag rug to take a nap. I remember such cold days when I could not go to school because the roads were drifted shut and the bus could not get through. Mother sewed or mended clothes, we girls read or sewed. I started a quilt from the small scraps my grandmother Griffith had left over from the one she was making, and worked on it for several years. (It was not finished until about 1975, when I was living in Cincinnati, and I finally got it out and finished it for Anne, my youngest daughter.)

The water tanks for the livestock froze in such weather, and had to be kept warm with a special kind of heater—a tank heater. A fire of corn cobs or wood burned down inside an immersible heater, and had to be fed often. The poor chickens were housed in an old building that was just an outer shell of wood, and often they would have frozen combs. Unless the eggs were gathered several times a day they would be frozen, and warm water had to be taken to the henhouse more often, because it would soon cool and freeze.

Some winters we had so much snow that we couldn't use the car—and what plow equipment the county owned in those days never came near us. We were on the county line and too far away from De Smet. The wheels were removed from the basic wagon, and heavy sled runners were fastened on instead—then we had a bob-sled. When we went to town in the winter in the sled, triple boxes were stacked on the sled, and benches were placed in thick straw inside. That is the way we rode. We had coarse, heavy blankets and the fur robe to put around us, and perhaps hot rocks to warm our feet.

I think what I disliked most about the bitterest cold of winter was having to go out to the privy, a few yards from the house. Here the cold drafts blew up around my bare bottom, and the mound of excrement froze into a solid mountain underneath. The alternative to going out to the privy was to use the slop jar in the house and then carry it out and dump it, and I disliked that even more than going out to the outhouse in the first place.

The stoves had to be fed wood constantly during the day, but the two in the living room and dining room would hold a fire overnight if a large log of ash was put on late in the evening. After school, I would empty the ashes, carry them out and dump them over the fence into the pigpen. It always amazed me to see the pigs crunching bits of wood charcoal and wood ash—I wondered what appetite it satisfied, and how they knew it was good for them!

As I think back now, I don't remember emptying ashes and carrying wood as a hard, dreary task—what I mostly remember are the glorious winter sunsets that I often enjoyed. I would climb on top of the stack of railroad ties or the corn crib to watch the ever-changing colors of the western sky, and sit there until I grew chilled and had to go back inside.

Smells are important triggers of memory, and even now, the smell of mown grass that has dried in the sun can evoke the memory of the haymow in winter. In the cow barn—the old barn—the smell in the haymow was of alfalfa, which could always remind me of a hot summer day in the hayfield.

One cold winter night we had a frightening experience with fire. Supper was over and we were all sitting around the dining room table, with homework, the daily paper, and the radio. There was a strong northwest wind blowing the snow into new drifts. Suddenly we heard a roaring sound. Dad knew what it was—the chimney was burning out! The buildup of creosote inside the brick chimney that started in the basement was on fire, and we all rushed outside to see the flames shooting high into the sky.

Dad didn't seem to worry too much about the house catching on fire (or perhaps he was good at concealing his fear from us) but he worried about the wind carrying the sparks to the woodpile, which was directly in the path of the wind. He and Uncle Bliss kept a close watch on the woodpile and the house roof until the flames had died down, but there was enough blowing snow to put out all of the sparks. If the wind had been from a different direction, the house might have burned down, because there was no way we could have saved it.

10

Everyone Pitches In

Making hay was hot, hard work, and had not improved a whole lot in terms of physical labor over the days of the hand scythe and rake. True, mowing machines and horse-drawn rakes made greater production possible, but a man (or woman) with a pitchfork still was needed. We girls and Mom were all called to lend a hand.

Mom usually drove the team on the buck rake when there was alfalfa to stack, while Dad and Uncle Bliss did the stacking. I helped pitch the hay up onto the stack for Dad or Uncle Bliss, who knew how to place it in such a way that the stack could be rounded off on top, in order to settle and shed water.

Some of the alfalfa was hauled in and stored in the haymow of the old barn, to be fed to the milk cows in the winter. Usually there was more alfalfa than the barn would hold, and the excess was stacked outside.

A buck rake is a hard machine to describe. It was a wide set of long, wooden, metal-capped teeth that slid forward along the ground and under the haycocks, which had been piled up by a horse-drawn rake. The buck rake was pulled by two horses hitched separately, wide apart, one at each side of the rake. Several haycocks would be gathered onto the wooden teeth and then driven to the stack. The team was then backed off, leaving the pile beside the stack, ready to be pitched up onto the top.

Timothy hay, which was fed to the horses, was stored in the horse barn, and most of the crop could be stored in the large haymow. My help was more likely to be needed when the haymow was being filled.

The farm had two hayracks, because at threshing time both Dad and Uncle Bliss used one. The man-hours of work needed to do the job at each farm were tallied, and a farmer with a larger threshing job paid his neighbors for the extra hours. Our farm usually had the longer job, and two men working evened it out somewhat.

When they hauled the hay into the barn, both racks were used, filled in the field, and driven in to be stowed in the loft. Before they were taken to the field, a "sling", which resembled a hammock, was laid in the bottom of a hayrack, the ends fastened front and back. Another sling was carried along. In the field, the horses pulled the rack from haycock to haycock with very little verbal direction from the men, and Dad and Uncle Bliss pitched the hay into the rack. My job was to arrange it evenly in order to get the maximum amount on a load. When the rack was nearly filled, the second sling was laid over the hay, with the rope ends dangling front and back. The load was piled high and driven to the barn. I always liked the ride home on top of a high-piled load of sweet-smelling Timothy hay.

Back at the barn, the large door in the peak had been let down in readiness, and the hayrack was placed directly below it. The two ends of the top sling were hooked to a rope which hung from a pulley in the peak of the barn high above. Meanwhile, the team of horses were hitched by a doubletree to a heavy rope which was stretched along the barn floor to the opposite (north) end, up the north wall, and across the length of the peak of the barn roof to the pulley at the south end. When the team was driven away from the barn, the rope pulled the two ends of the sling together, and the hay began to lift, as in a basket, up to the peak of the roof. From here it moved along a track in the barn roof until it reached the spot where the men wanted to dump the hay. One of them then pulled on a light rope which released one end of the sling, and the hay dropped into the loft below.

The big haymow was always hot in the summertime, and pigeons and sparrows made their nests in the rafters and on the ceiling track. These nests and droppings often clogged the tracks and fouled the ropes, and had to be cleaned out before the lift would work. When the new crop of hay was put in, the loft had the good summer smell of grass and sun.

The bottom slingful of hay was lifted in the same way, and then the second haywagon. The big loft, when full, held enough hay to feed 12-14 horses until the next summer. Sometimes, when the weather was cooler, we played in the hayloft, climbing over the hay piled high near the roof in the center, and sliding down the steep sides.

In the winter, dusk came early, and it was dim in the barn by the time Dad finished the chores. I still remember "helping" my Dad feed the horses when I was little, and I felt proud to be big enough to fill and carry the pans of oats. All around, we could hear the contented horses munching hay and oats, and sometimes going "whoosh" into their feed boxes to blow out the oat kernels from the corners to where their tongues could reach them.

Almost every farm had a windmill to supply power to the water pump. I don't know whether ours was there when Grandpa bought the farm or whether he had it installed, but I'm guessing that he had the well drilled and the windmill put up. Dad and Uncle Bliss remembered the shallow well in the ravine below the barn as if they had used it.

I used to go to sleep in the summertime listening to the occasional "clang" of the windmill. I don't think the men usually left it pumping all night, but even when it was shut off and the fan turned out of the wind, the shutoff cable would bang against the tower, or the fan or wheel would move in the breeze. When it was pumping, it made a rhythmical clang that was steady and reassuring.

Shallow wells weren't too satisfactory in eastern South Dakota. The artesian well that the windmill pumped was about 350 feet deep. Farther west, the water table was closer to the surface or more powerful, and there were artesian wells that flowed to the surface. The Capitol Lake beside the Statehouse in Pierre is fed by a flowing well, and the constant flame that burns above the flow is fed by the natural gas that comes up with the water.

Two large oblong, square-bottomed wood water troughs stood at right angles to each other in the feeding lot beside our windmill. A water tank for the hogs stood by the fence where the feed lots joined, and all could be filled by connecting different pipes to the pump. The wooden horse troughs were built of heavy planks with two 4 x 4's across the top of each. I remember the one time new ones had to be built, and I wondered how they would hold water. But as soon as they were filled, they swelled and were water-tight.

Most of the time there was plenty of wind to pump water for all the stock, but there were some times when the wind failed. Then the small gasoline engine, which did so many jobs, was again put into service. It was moved into the "engine house" (or pump-house/tool shed) beside the windmill and hitched to the well pump by a belt that ran through a small doorway in the side of the shed. The belt ran a "pump jack", which worked the pump.

Every few years, the stream of water coming from the pump would thin out and indicate a need to pull the sand point. Then Dad would call in a well-drilling company to do the job. They came with a powered lift which they fastened to the windmill frame, and with this they pulled up section after section of the pump pipe, and leaned them against the inside of the tower. Each had to be uncoupled from the one below as they came up. The last section to be raised was the short sieve-like section of pipe that ended in a solid point—the sand point. When it emerged from the well, it was always rusty and solidly packed with sand—like cement. A new sand point stood ready to be lowered; a section of pump pipe was attached to it, and all the sections were put back into the well. Then the pump worked like new.

Somewhere during this whole operation, the men always brought up perhaps a pailful of clean white sand, like none that I have seen anywhere else except on the Gulf-Coast beaches at St. Joseph's Peninsula, Florida. I claimed this sand for my playhouse. It was such a wonderful surprise to come from the depths of the earth, and it made me think about all of the layers of earth and stone and sand and clay that we couldn't see.

I cannot remember the exact date that the old well gave out. The water was still there, but the metal pipe that was the well casing had deteriorated or collapsed. It must have been about 1940. I wasn't home when they had the new one drilled, just a few feet from the old.

I remember the well-driller as Will Blakewell, whose son was in my class at school in Erwin; Evelyn remembers the Frahm Brothers. No matter. The engine-house/tool shed had to be moved a few feet south, and it was during that move that our little rat terrier dog, Tyke, had his greatest moment—killing rats.

One year during the drought, Dad and Uncle Bliss dug a pit silo beside the cow barn with the idea of turning Russian thistles, which grew plentifully around the farm, into usable feed. It was supposed to be something like silage after storage in a silo, but their experiment wasn't successful.

The men's efforts were not a total loss, however, for the pit made a good garbage dump. With no sewer system, waste water and garbage were always a problem—one that no one wanted to deal with. Usually the slop pail under the wash sink in the kitchen collected everything, and was emptied behind the coal shed, with the consequence that the ground there always smelled sour and only coarse weeds would grow in that spot. Cans and bottles landed there, too, to be raked up every so often and hauled away to a dumping area back in a field by the railroad tracks. Before the days of rendering plants, dead farm animals would also be hauled there, in winter when the ground was frozen. They would be covered with straw or manure and left for the weather and wild animals to dispose of.

The pit silo made an ideal garbage dump. Trash and garbage didn't have to be hauled so far, and it gradually filled up. I remember that when old Sally, Grandpa's white driving pony, got too old and ill to eat, the silo made a handy grave. Dad and Uncle Bliss took her to the side of the pit and ended her life with a rifle shot. It was easy then to cover her with earth. I think the silo became a grave for at least one more old horse. The afternoon that the old pony was shot, I took a long, slow walk to the mailbox—I didn't want even to hear the sound of the shot that ended the life of Sally-Walk-Around-The-Barn!

Sometime around 1941, the old chicken house was torn down and a new one built, this one with a good cement floor that would keep out badgers and skunks. Several times they had dug under the floor of the old building and killed quite a few chickens. I can remember attacking the old chicken house to tear it down. There was something very satisfactory in "shoveling" off the old shingles with a spade, and pulling apart the sides with a crowbar!

I remember waking one morning when I was about five or six years old to the strong smell of skunk close by. Dad had set a trap to see if he could catch the skunk that had been getting into the chickens for a couple of nights, and he had caught it, but by a leg only. A very angry skunk had let us know its situation! Dad went out with his rifle and shot it, and then he dug a hole with a post-hole digger close by the animal, pushed the carcass in, and quickly covered it. It was some time, though, before the aroma was entirely gone, especially around the chicken house.

Badgers were another problem in the chicken house. I have a special memory of a badger from when I was only four or five. Dad came in from the field one evening and said that he had seen a fresh badger hole under the fence at the back of the pasture. He thought it wouldn't be long before the animal began to raid the chicken house, and he decided to shoot it before it had a chance.

That evening he took a gun, and taking me by the hand, walked across the pasture. We sat down on the grass near the badger hole and waited quietly. I don't remember waiting very long until the badger poked its nose out of the hole, then came out, sat up and looked around, sniffing the air. Dad took careful aim and shot it. He must have known something of the habits of badgers to have guessed correctly when it would appear. As I think back on that evening, it seems rather strange for him to have taken me along, but I accepted it as perfectly normal, and went happily with him. It seemed like a play, with Dad, the badger, and me all playing our parts! I was not overly disturbed with the killing of the badger—it was something that had to be done. When I was a little older, I had a badger fur muff that I liked very much, but it didn't come from that badger.

Corn raised for fodder was planted in rows, like it is today, rather than in hills equidistant apart. That was called "checked" corn planting. Fodder corn was not planted to produce ears, but to produce an abundance of small stalks and leaves, with some ears. It was cut with a grain binder which tied it into bundles with twine. These were shocked in the field until they were dry enough to be hauled in to the barnyard and stacked for winter feed. The cattle looked first for the ears in the fodder, and afterward ate the leaves and stalks. The milk cows received an extra ration of alfalfa hay in their mangers when they were let in to their stalls for milking.

The "checked" corn, planted to produce a better crop of ears, was picked by hand until Dad and Uncle Bliss bought the corn picker in partnership with our closest neighbor, John Hinders. John's son, Harm, was often hired to pick corn before they bought the picker, and Dad and Uncle Bliss also picked. It seems to me that they usually were able to pick a triple-box wagonload of ear corn in half a day. Nowadays the skill of hand-picking corn is almost lost, although a few men compete in contests at fairs. Plowing with a horse-drawn plow is another contest whose purpose is to teach young people "how it used to be done."

Back to the corn. We didn't have a special building for a corn crib, but the men always set up circles of "cribbing", which was fencing made of vertical wood slats held in place and spaced a couple of inches apart by wire twisted around them. A couple of fence posts stabilized the crib until it was full of corn and also provided an opening for shoveling out the corn when needed. Often, when the first circle was full, a second circle of cribbing was placed on top of it. These temporary structures held the corn that was fed to the pigs and steers in the hog pen.

When Dad was ready to plant "checked corn", he first stretched a special wire across one side of the field. This wire had knots spaced about every two feet along its length, and it stretched from a heavy spool at one end, across the field and through the eye or loop of an iron stake at the other end, then back to another stake at the beginning. He threaded this wire through a slot in the corn planter, filled the two canisters (it was a two-row planter) with seed corn and drove the team across the field. At the other end he moved the stake over the distance of two rows and made another trip across and back. Each round trip planted four rows, evenly spaced when the knots in the wire tripped the discs in the bottom of the canisters. When the corn came up, it could be seen in rows from either the side or the end of the field. It was cultivated three times while it was young, twice in one direction and the second time at right angles to the other two.

Nowadays, hybrid seed corn and fertilizers produce double or more of the crops Dad used to raise, even when it is planted thicker and in continuous rows like other grains. It seems to me that quite a bit of skill was necessary to plant a perfectly-spaced field of "checked corn" that could be cultivated both ways.

My sister Evelyn recalls how Dad used to check the germination of his seed corn. He would select 100 kernels of corn from the ears on the racks in the haymow and place them on damp blotting paper or flannel on an old pie pan. Damp paper or flannel was laid over the top and another pie pan used for a cover. The seed started was placed in a warm place, and when the kernels sprouted, he could figure out the percentage of fertility. If he didn't think it good enough, he would buy some other seed. I think the planter put about 4 kernels in each hill—"One for the blackbird, one for the crow, one for the gopher, and one to grow!"

Stormy Weather

The stock market crash in 1929 had its effect, bringing low prices for farm products, but it didn't affect us as much as it did people in the cities. Farmers didn't lose their jobs, and we mostly raised enough to eat. I do remember, somewhere about this time, selling eggs for 11¢ a dozen and buying gasoline for 19¢ a gallon.

The "Bank Holiday" of 1932, declared by President Franklin Roosevelt right after he took office in the midst of the nationwide banking crisis, was a greater calamity to our farm family than the stock market crash—because Uncle Bliss lost $3000. Dad had little in his checking or savings account, because he had just paid taxes. Evelyn and I had a few dollars each in savings. We had drawn out $12.50 each a year or so before to buy Grandpa Ackley his radio when he was going blind from cataracts and could no longer read the paper. When the banks closed, we were glad that the money had been spent for Grandpa's radio, because we ended up losing only about $7 or $8 apiece.

Bliss eventually received some compensation for his lost savings, when the holding company that handled the bank's affairs paid him in horses that they had taken in foreclosure from someone else. I don't think he ever received the full value of his lost savings, but he got Barney and Jack, and Dick and Dolly, two teams of horses greatly needed for farm work until they gave way to a tractor a few years later.

On 21 March 1933, Grandpa and Grandma celebrated 50 years of marriage. Grandpa was getting quite frail and didn't want a social gathering, so it was celebrated with a special dinner at their home in Bryant. Only his family was present, but Uncle Carl came from Montana with his youngest son, Clarence, and that made the occasion special.

I remember that Clarence, and probably Dorothy, became tired and cross, and Grandpa was upset by their crying in the small house. He retreated to the basement until the children settled down.

Oklahoma didn't have all of the dust storms in the middle 1930s. We had our share. They always came out of the west, in the late afternoon. The first signs were a quickening of the wind, a line of dark clouds along the horizon, and then a mist of fine dust particles in the air. As the storm clouds built higher, they rolled and tumbled over each other, deep gray and blue-black.

The sky grew darker, the air thicker, and we all shut ourselves indoors to wait out another storm. The worst ones turned the day into night. One time we tried pulling one window shade and leaving another one up, and one view was as black as the other.

Anyone who had to be outside—either because he was caught in the storm too far from home, or had to rescue chickens or pets—kept a bandana handy to tie over his face to screen out a little of the dust. Farmers who were caught in their fields sometimes lost direction and wandered far away from the safety of the barn. Most farmers in our area still used horse-power, and even the horses could become completely disoriented.

As a storm built up, the force of the wind increased and the noise was deafening. We tried packing wet towels and rags around the windows to help keep out as much of the finest particles as possible, but inside the house the air was still thick with dust, and our throats felt dry. A couple of years of drought had dried out the houses, and there were plenty of cracks and spaces.

I remember one particular time when the wind had risen very quickly, and we looked outside to see chickens being blown by the wind until they reached some barrier that stopped them. Usually it was a fence, and they were caught there, along with the Russian thistles that tumbled with them. They were in danger of being buried in dust against the fence. I put on a jacket, a wet bandana over my face, bandit style, and a leather aviator-type helmet on my head, and went out to battle the wind and rescue the chickens. I did succeed in saving the chickens, but I was very glad to get back in the house.

Fences filled up with thistles, as the thistles rolled and skipped before the wind until some barrier stopped them. The embedded thistles held the topsoil that blew off the fields, and each succeeding storm added to the accumulation until only the tops of the fence posts could be seen, and the mass settled down and packed so hard that the cattle could walk right over them. It was many years before all of these buried fences were dug out.

We and our neighbors endured, and in order to relieve the monotony, we planned neighborhood parties in our homes, with card playing or dancing and singing to a neighbor's fiddle or mandolin—these cost little money.

I remember especially one time when the gathering was to be at our house. We had cleaned upstairs and down and warmed the whole house (we didn't heat the upstairs in winter). In the late afternoon, the familiar dark clouds rolled up in the west and we had a bad storm. When it was over, the pattern of the green linoleum in the west bedroom upstairs could not be seen—it was covered with dust and even fine pieces of grass.

Mom sat down and cried. Later, when she swept it up, she filled a pill bottle full of the sweepings. She mailed that bottle to a pen-friend, to show her just what a prairie dust storm could do and to help explain what we were up against.

Mother had always enjoyed writing letters to pen friends as well as distant relatives, and one of the small luxuries she allowed herself, even when times were the hardest, was 3¢ stamps. She had pen friends in several states in different parts of the country, and looked forward to their letters telling about their families and how they lived.

One pen-friendship repaid with more than friendship the time and money Mom spent on it. Vera and Joe Steele, of Matamoras, Pennsylvania, were interested in farm life on the prairie, so different from their small city, near New York City. When the drought and dust storms came, and times were desperate for us, they decided they could help. Vera read Mom's letters to her friends, and showed them the small bottle of dust and chaff which Mom had sent her—that sample of what we had swept up off a bedroom floor after one particularly bad dust storm. They wrote back to ask if we would mind if they sent some things to help out.

Those packages were better than Christmas! We received one from a drugstore, with toothpaste and brushes, band-aids, aspirin, a thermometer—all the necessities we might buy there. Another was from a woman who worked in a garment factory making girls' slips, nightgowns, and panties. She sent ends of bolts of material, and finished tops of slips and nightgowns. We made bras and panties for several years from that material.

Best of all were the boxes of clothing—we never knew what treasures might appear when we opened them! We all remember a leather aviator's helmet that we had fun wearing, and skirts and dresses and coats. The two winter coats I wore in college were "made over" from some in those packages.

As the drought worsened, all of the reserves of our family were exhausted. Both Bliss and Dad applied for WPA work but were turned down the first time because they owned the farm. No matter that it had not produced enough to keep us and our livestock alive.

Finally regulations were changed, and Dad was allowed $40 per month plus "commodities" for working a certain number of hours every month hauling gravel and spreading it on roads. For him, I think this was the most degrading experience of his life, and he became silent and morose, or cursed the drought and the government. We ate the canned goods we were issued, but no amount of camouflage could make that canned mutton very appetizing.

Although there wasn't a lot of money, the farm took care of its family until the years of drought and dust storms, and those disastrous years of 1934 to 1936 almost ruined it.

For three of four years, crops were sparse because of low rainfall; one year it took only half a day for the threshing machine to finish our crop, and the next year we raised nothing at all. There was no feed for livestock, and all but the horses and half a dozen milk cows were sold. The garden produced nothing, and my mother's attempt to fence off a part of the hog pen near the well in order to have a garden spot she could irrigate didn't work. Perhaps the soil was too poor, or perhaps they didn't know enough about irrigation.

It was during this time that Dad and Uncle Bliss tried to make use of the abundant green Russian thistles, which were supposed to make silage—good livestock feed. (I have since read that thistles are high in protein.) They dug a pit silo near the feed lot and mowed thistles and packed them into it. But the cattle didn't like them and the silage spoiled. The few milk cows gave us some cream to sell, and the chickens produced a few dozen eggs each week, and for a while that was our only income.

When times were worst, the radio was put away, and the newspaper—The Daily Argus-Leader from Sioux Falls—was cancelled. The telephone was kept, except for a year or so, because it was the link with the grandparents in Bryant.

In 1934, when the grain and corn had shriveled in the heat, the State Relief Administration urged the planting of millet and cane for feed crops. On June 6, Uncle Bliss either purchased, or was allotted, from the South Dakota State Relief Administration: 75 lbs of Amber Cane, 27 lbs of Sudan Grass, and 75 lbs of Proso Millet.

I don't remember if these crops grew and matured that year or not. However, for some years after this, until the drought seemed finally in the past, the men planted these hardy, quick-maturing crops for feed.

These years of the middle 1930s were the low point for our farm and the family. The hot winds blew almost every day—we could never get away from them. There was just no place of cool that we could retreat to, and at night we welcomed the twilight time when the winds died down. We would sit on the rough cement back steps, wash our feet in a basin of warm water and dry them on old towels, and enjoy a breeze that felt soft and soothing after the harsh day. After we rigged up the shower in the old smoke house, we girls and Dad would take a shower in the evening with water that had warmed in the sun all afternoon on the back steps.

Another scourge during the middle 1930s was the grasshopper plague. I don't remember exactly which years they were the worst, but it could not have been the year that we raised nothing at all. They also came out of the west, or so it seemed, and some days we could look upward to see glittering clouds of them, carried by the wind to wherever the wind slackened and let them down to earth. Their wings reflected the sun like many tiny lights.

The state and county governments attempted to fight back at the plague of grasshoppers by spreading poisoned bran mixed with molasses around the edges of the fields of green corn at the time the corn was most likely to be attacked. We drove the old car around the edges of the fields, stopping to put small amounts at regular intervals. We didn't have enough to deposit a continuous trail of it. We had a container in the car that we dipped it out of, and we had to be especially careful not to get any of it on our hands or clothes. The son of our veterinarian died as a result of helping to mix the bran. The story was that he had athlete's foot and some of the mixture soaked through his shoes.

We never thought that the poison bran really did much good, but it was one way of fighting back.

At this time, our family was grateful for the tree claim—all mature ash trees now—and the railroad. Discarded railroad ties and the hardwood from the ash grove kept us warm in winter in three wood stoves, sometimes four when it got so cold that a fire had to be lit in the cellar to keep the potatoes and canned goods from freezing. The men would mark the dead trees in the summer, cut them in the winter, haul them home and saw them into stove lengths with a circular saw powered by a gasoline engine. I'll never forget the sound of that old "one-lunger" engine, with its irregular firing. During those years, my after-school job was to clean out the ashes from a couple of the stoves and carry in wood for the next day.

In 1935, our cousin Phyllis Ackley, who lived in the tiny town of Medora, North Dakota, came to stay with Grandma and Grandpa Ackley in Bryant to finish high school, in order to be able to take the required subjects her home school didn't offer for college entrance. She was a senior in Bryant, and I in Erwin. This also helped the grandparents, for Uncle Carl sent board money every month. Grandma also boarded another high school girl whose parents brought produce. In this way our grandparents managed when the farm could provide almost no help or income for them.

But the fall school term had hardly begun in 1935 when Grandpa Ackley died in his home on September 9, aged 81 years (he was born in 1854). He had suffered from asthma almost all of his life, and had been blind, or nearly so, for the last four or five years. He was laid out in his casket in the parlor of his small home in Bryant, and buried from the Congregational Church. A quartet sang a favorite hymn—"Let the Lower Lights Be Burning"—at his funeral. He was buried in the same plot as Sarah, Dad's first wife, in the Erwin Cemetery.

In the spring of 1936, both Phyllis and I graduated from high school, and she went home to Medora. Dad and Mother felt that Grandma should not be living alone in Bryant, and the only place to take her was to the farm. I am sure she would rather have stayed in Bryant, where her house had more modern conveniences, but she didn't protest too much. I remember that summer as a very pleasant one, having Grandma with us.

I was beginning to sew for myself, and was pleased to make Grandma a couple of summer dresses. She occupied the downstairs bedroom again, as she had when she came from Illinois. As I look back now, I feel sorry when I remember that Grandma lived in a really comfortable house, with a furnace, electricity, and a bathroom, for only about 10 years of her whole life!

I left home in the fall to work in De Smet for the sum of $3 per week and my room and board. I first worked for a family where the mother was the breadwinner, a nurse for the Child Welfare Department of the State, and later for a family who ran a dairy farm. There I encountered my first sex discrimination in wages—when I asked for a raise, contending that I worked just as hard as the hired man, who received $30 per month, I was informed that if I were staying on and not leaving to go to college, they would have considered it.

On 1 February 1937, Mary Ida (Maxwell) Ackley (born in 1859) died of a stroke at the farm. She had been ill for about a month, and during that time I had not seen her, because that was a winter of heavy snow and many blizzards, and I had not been home since Christmas. I managed to get home for the funeral, by taking a train from De Smet the 10 miles east to Lake Preston, and then riding in the freight caboose from there to Bryant, about 20 miles north. One of my uncles took me in his car to the farm, on a road which the neighbors had opened through the drifts with shovels; but that night we had another storm, and all the roads were drifted shut again.

If anyone had taken a picture of our family going to town for the funeral, it would have looked like pioneer times, for we went in a bob-sled, bundled up in blankets and an old fur robe that we had used for many years. It had been made from the hide of a black horse before I was born, and in one place it still had the longer hair of the mane. When we reached our Ackley grandparents' home in Bryant, the horses were put into the garage out of the wind, or were left outside wearing the blankets we had been wrapped in.

Grandma was buried in Woodlawn Cemetery at Bryant, because, when Grandpa was buried in Erwin Cemetery, it was found that the two other gravesites on the plot had been usurped by another family, and there was no more room there. Dad and Uncle Bliss talked of moving Grandpa's grave to Woodlawn, but money was scarce, and somehow it was never done.

Grandpa had left a will, leaving the farm to Grandma, and to each of his sons, $100. I don't remember if he had any money from which the hundred dollars could be paid. Grandma decided to deed the farm to her sons while she was living, in order to avoid probate expenses at her death, but the family was in deep financial trouble. Taxes for several years were delinquent, and they amounted to more than $600 on the northwest quarter alone. Through a friend at the bank, Dad learned that there was a man in Lake Preston interested in buying the farm for taxes, but Dad could not face that. He was able to arrange a bank loan for $1600, and the taxes were paid, but crops were not good again in 1936. My memory of the situation is that Dad borrowed on his life insurance to make up the difference to pay the mortgage.

A friend of our family offered to lend me money to go to college, and I accepted her offer and enrolled in Eastern State Normal School at Madison, South Dakota. Times were still hard, but most of my classmates were in the same circumstances.

Dad and Mom drove to Madison, taking me and my belongings, and I was installed in a room in East Hall, the women's dorm. I had a single room both of the years I was there—cost, $6 per month. I do not remember exactly, but the $600 I borrowed paid for tuition and board, at least for that year. Books were furnished, the same as in the public schools.

I enjoyed my two years at Eastern (now Dakota State University, still teaching young people how to be teachers, but also emphasizing computer technology even more). I made good friends there, and have kept in touch with some of them ever since. I think my favorite classes were journalism and literature. It was there I first came to know the Laura Ingalls Wilder books, in a class in Children's Literature.

In 1939, Uncle Carl died in Glendive, Montana. Aunt Nellie and the younger children soon moved to Seattle, Washington, where prospects for jobs were better. During the war, Aunt Nellie and some of the cousins worked at the Boeing Aircraft Company there.

After completing my studies, I accepted a contract to teach 5th and 6th grades and supervise the high school newspaper at Onida, South Dakota, and I went there by train in early September 1939. Dad took me to De Smet, where I boarded the train for Redfield. At Redfield, I took another train to Onida. There the local drayman hauled my trunk to the hotel, where I had rented a room, along with four other teachers in a separate wing in back of the lobby.

After that, I was only a resident of the farm in the summertime. I would come home from my teaching job and help with whatever was being done—canning, sewing, doing the chores, helping with the harvest.

Dad was hospitalized with a duodenal ulcer in 1940. The years of worry about the farm and family and money and crops took their toll. He was never a man who could talk about his problems—he kept it all inside. After a stay in the Huron hospital, he came home and gradually regained strength on a careful diet.

In 1941, the appearance of the farm changed somewhat, when a shelterbelt—a dozen rows of several kinds of trees, half a mile long—was planted north of the farm buildings and garden. These trees were planted by an agency of the government which was encouraging all landowners to plant trees to replace those which had died during the drought. These trees would also help to break the constant winds which blew from the northwest and help keep the soil from blowing away. Our old tree claim had been our warmth during the dry years, and Dad thought it was a good idea.

Although teams of men from the government agency planted the trees, they were our responsibility after that. They had to be hoed that first year, to keep weeds from choking out the tiny trees, and cultivated like corn. A variety of trees were planted: cottonwood, of course, because it grew quickly; Chinese elm and Russian olive, for their hardiness; some evergreens along the protected south side. Some hybrid varieties of sand cherry, Nanking cherry, and plums were also planted along the south side, to provide hardy fruit for birds and humans.

Evelyn graduated from high school in 1941, and left in the fall to go to Eastern State Normal School, to take the two-year teacher's course. We both came back to the farm in the summers to help with canning and harvest.

My fiancé, Edwin Johnson, whom I had met after I began teaching in Onida, had his introduction to the farm the summer that the shelterbelt was new. He came to visit, and helped hoe the young trees.

Edwin joined the armed forces when war was on the horizon. He came home on leave from Camp Pickett, Virginia, and we were married in the Congregational Church in Bryant on 27 June 1943. That summer I didn't help on the farm, but spent it in Blackstone, Virginia, near Camp Pickett. He went overseas in October of that year, and I went back to teach another year in Onida.

Crops were good again, and we had several busy summers. No new machinery was available, and threshing was still done with a "separator" powered by an old gasoline engine.

On the day that Japan asked for peace, in August 1945—effectively ending World War II—I was running the tractor and Dad was on the binder behind, and we were cutting flax in the north field, on the county line.

We had all been expecting news of the surrender of Japan, and we waited impatiently for it to be broadcast on the radio. About the middle of the afternoon, Evelyn rode out to the field on the bicycle to let us know that it had just been announced. I think this was the last time I was ever on a tractor doing farm work, because Edwin came home that November and we lived in Onida for the next four years.

12

As Time Goes By

Evelyn's fiancé, Ed Christensen, came home from his military service shortly before Christmas 1945. They were married on 28 December, in the Congregational Church in Bryant that we Ackley girls had attended for many years. After they were married, they went to Ashland, Wisconsin, where Ed finished his interrupted college course. Later, they both taught in Wisconsin.

About this time, Mom and Dad decided to make a major improvement in the old, cramped farm kitchen. Mom had raised and sold chickens, geese, and eggs for some years, and used some of the money to help make improvements. Now she wanted the kitchen enlarged, new cupboards, a new stove, a sink with a pump, and a large window on the east side over the sink. About this time, the Rural Electric lines were put in past the house and Dad had the house wired.

This brought more conveniences—a refrigerator, an electric radio, a wool rug in the living room with a vacuum cleaner to clean it, and, best of all, electric lights! No more smelly kerosene lamps with smoky chimneys, no more Aladdin lamp over the table in the dining room, with its fragile mantel which disintegrated if you were too rough. And with a hand pump over the sink in the kitchen, water no longer had to be carried into the house—but it still had to be carried out!

After so many years of having its paint scoured off by wind and dust, the house was painted white again. Dad had a cement floor poured in the basement and new shelves built to hold Mom's canned produce—fruit and vegetables, pickles and jelly and catsup. The potato bin remained, and every winter potatoes were stored in it, but the huge stone jars were no longer used for curing meat. The pigs were now taken to a butcher, who cut them up and made the ham and bacon, and stored it all in his freezer until it was needed.

A few years before all this, the heating stoves in the dining room and living room yielded to a bottle gas furnace, which was placed in an enlarged doorway between the two rooms. The old Monarch kitchen "range" was also discarded in favor of a gas cookstove. The hot water reservoir at the side of the old stove was sorely missed, however, and Mom soon added a small wood stove, with a large kettle to sit on top and warm a supply of water any time the weather was cool enough to require a little warmth in the kitchen.

We tried to persuade Dad to put in a sewer system, but he was sure that the deep clay underlying the black topsoil would not drain properly and would present too many problems, so he would not consider it. The old privy was moved again and again.

Another improvement was a new two-car garage and tool shed near the house. The old tool shed had been moved from beside the windmill to a location farther south, but this move weakened the building, and it began to lean and finally fell down.

Dorothy finished high school in 1947 and went to Minneapolis to attend business school.

In April of 1949, Edwin and I adopted a three-month-old baby girl and named her Linda Carol. When she was 5 months old, Mother suffered a stroke and was hospitalized in Huron. Dorothy came home to run the house and take care of Mother, and Linda and I spent three weeks at the farm to help, and to try to interest Grandma in her new granddaughter.

Dorothy married Harold Sauder on 2 October 1949, and they took over part of the farm with Uncle Bliss. Mom and Dad moved to Bryant to live in the small house that Grandpa Ackley had bought in 1924.

In the fall of 1950, the farm sheltered a member of the fourth generation of Ackleys, when Gene Sauder was born to Dorothy and Harold. He was joined by his brother Jerry in 1951. In the spring of 1952, Dorothy and Harold rented a farm of their own, northwest of Bryant.

That left Uncle Bliss alone on the farm.

Uncle Bliss had always lived with some of his family, first his parents and brothers, then with our family, and finally with Dorothy and Harold. It seemed to me that after they left, he rather enjoyed being the master of his own house, able to do what he wanted to when he wanted to. He cared for the cattle, and for the dogs and cats. He cooked the way he liked. But he didn't do much cleaning except to wash his dishes, and the house soon showed neglect.

Income from the farm paid the taxes, and Social Security took care of his food and clothing. He sold the old wooden churn, the mantel clock, and some parts of the old 1928 Chevy to an antique dealer, and we girls took some of the old books, crocks, and utensils that reminded us of our childhood. By 1950 both Evelyn and Ed, and Edwin and I had moved to Cincinnati, Ohio, and came back some summers to visit.

Mom and Dad lived about two years in Bryant before Dad was stricken with appendicitis. He had an operation in St. John's Hospital in Huron, but my Dad, Leslie Edward Ackley, born in 1886, died on 20 August 1951 of peritonitis from the ruptured appendix.

After Dad's death, Mom spent two winters with my family in Cincinnati, often visiting with my sister Evelyn and her husband Ed. She enjoyed her granddaughters, my daughters Linda Carol (born in 1949) and baby Christine Leslie (born in 1951) in our home, and grandson Peter Christensen, Evelyn's son, who was born in February 1952.

After her two winters in Cincinnati, Mother felt stronger and able to stay by herself in her own home. She spent the winter of 1953–54 in Bryant, closer to more of her friends and relatives. She entertained friends for Easter Sunday dinner, 1954, and then died peacefully in her sleep that night. My Mother, Verna Mae Griffith, born in 1894, is buried beside Dad and Grandma Mary Ida in Woodlawn Cemetery at Bryant.

After Mom's death, I had two more children, Mark William born in 1955 and Anne Helen born in 1956. (My firstborn, Curtis Lee, was born in 1947 but died within a few days.) My sister Evelyn had three sons: Peter Edward Christensen born 1952, John Ackley Christensen born 1954, and David Loken Christensen born 1956. Dorothy had five children: Gene Harold Sauder born 1950, Jerry Dean Sauder born 1951, Leanne Joy Sauder born 1955, Bonnie Patricia Sauder born 1956, and Jill Marie Sauder born 1967.

Uncle Bliss continued to live on the farm alone for 18 years. Gradually, he turned over more and more of the work to Harold and his sons. After the war, farming methods and machines changed. There were no more horses in the barn; tractors did the work, and they got bigger and bigger. Harvesting probably changed the most—combines went through the fields, cutting and threshing the ripe grain and emptying it into tractor-pulled wagons or trucks to be hauled to the elevator or stored in bins. Often the grain was cut, wind-rowed, and allowed to dry for a few days before being picked up and threshed by the combine. Fertilizers increased crop yields, and better seed helped produce more grain or corn per acre.

After Mother's death, my sisters and I sold the tree claim quarter section and the 80 acres next to it. We always visited the farm when we went to South Dakota, and were glad to see Uncle Bliss. Although we were sorry to see the house acquiring a smoky grime from the way he liked to fry hamburgers and steak on a very hot fire, we knew he would be upset if we tried to do anything about it. He enjoyed his television, he subscribed to a daily paper—and The Saturday Evening Post—and drove his blue pick-up truck to town or to Dorothy and Harold's. When the pick-up truck was still new, he and our cousin Leroy Houge drove it to Cincinnati and spent a week or so with us here. He came another time by train, and we all took turns taking him to the baseball games, which he really enjoyed.

Uncle Bliss began to suffer from emphysemia—he was a heavy smoker all of his life—and finally was hospitalized in De Smet for treatment. While there, he suffered two ruptured aneurysms, and died on 24 September 1969. Born in 1898, John Bliss Ackley is buried with his mother in Woodlawn Cemetery.

After that, the house stood empty and gradually deteriorated.

Some of the changes that took place during those years when Uncle Bliss lived alone on the farm would have been almost unbelievable to Grandma and Grandpa Ackley. They had become used to water from a faucet and a bathroom and electric lights in their home in Bryant, but they would not have believed that a water line would bring water through plastic pipes to the farm from wells miles away. Although the second deep well by the barn has now gone the way of the first, and the pond backed up by a dam in the pasture may go dry, the cattle can be watered by filling the tank from a faucet.

With the changes in farming after World War II, the old machinery was no longer used, and the old binders, hay rake, plows, a mower, and a grain drill all sat and rusted away, hidden in tall grass and weeds. The porch on the house sagged, and was pulled away from the house by the Virginia creeper vine which Mother had planted long ago to try to provide a little shade on the west side of the house. The mice worked unchecked in the few old books that were still left in the upstairs store room.

The shelterbelt that was planted in 1941 still stands, although the cottonwoods are mostly dead. Pines and sturdier trees remain, and other trees have sprung up from seeds. Deer and other wildlife seek shelter in them now. Uncle Bliss began to see deer on the farm in the 1960s, and they can often be spotted today.

Even while Bliss was still living, the farm had begun to look like a farm that nobody needed. The hog houses fell down, the granary sagged. Dorothy and Harold found use for the chicken house and the garage, and moved them to their farm on the outskirts of Bryant.

During the drought and depression years, there hadn't been enough money for gasoline to make any unnecessary trips, and often church was not essential. But on quiet clear mornings in the summer we could hear all of the church bells at the farm.

Now even the railroad is no more. The passenger trains stopped their twice-daily run through the farm soon after World War II, and the freight trains ran only a few years longer. Grain is hauled by truck to the large terminals.

In the summer of 1981, the tracks were being torn up and the rails and ties all sold. The right-of-way, which the first owner of the land sold to the first railroad company, was offered to the owners of adjoining land for something like $200 an acre. By 1989, all traces of the tracks were gone, and the embankment had been smoothed out to the level of the surrounding fields by bulldozers. You cannot get to Bryant by train any more.

The farm, as of 1990, is owned by my sister Dorothy Sauder and her son Jerry.

The last time I visited the farm, in the summer of 1989, still greater changes were apparent. The house had been torn down soon after Uncle Bliss's death, because much of the lumber in it was still good and usable. Strong timbers made the sills, and the square nails held it together. Gene Sauder used the lumber to build a garage, so it was not wasted.

Shortly before my visit, Dorothy and her family decided that the remaining old buildings on the farm, except for the big old horse barn, should be burned. This was done. The ashes and debris were smoothed away by a bulldozer.

While I was in South Dakota, I wondered if I wanted to see what was left of the place which was home for the first 25 years of my life. I thought it might make me too sad to see it with almost everything gone—the way I had seen four of the other farms we used to pass on our way to Bryant disappear. I decided that if I didn't go I would wonder about how it looked, so one afternoon Dorothy, Edwin, and I drove out there.

I was glad I did.

The scars of the burned buildings were already beginning to heal, and only the old red barn and the trees were left to mark the site. In the spot where I had dug up the tough sod for a flower garden when I was in high school, a few flowers still bloomed—bouncing bet and some scraggly iris. Two or three ash trees, which I planted as seedlings from the tree claim, had grown, and shaded what remained. The lilac hedge, which Mother and I planted from seedlings from the grandparents' home in Bryant, still flourishes along the hog pen fence. I never saw it bloom. The yellow rosebushes between my flower garden and the lilacs grow like wild ones.

Burning the old buildings had turned the farm back in time almost a hundred years. Some of the evidences of human habitation remain—the shelterbelt, fences, trees along the driveway, even a few old rhubarb and asparagus plants in the old garden, descendants of those planted at least 75 years ago—but the tall waving grass everywhere has healed the wounds. The old red horse barn leans tiredly away from the northwest winds, and will someday fall down and be burned like the other old buildings. But the wreck of a farm has healed.

Afterword

"Let's reminisce."

I heard these words often from my mother at family gatherings and Thanksgiving dinners when all the dishes had been cleared away.

Mom was a journalism teacher, and I think in the back of her mind she was always creating The Farm Story as she took the photos in this book. Her love of the farm, her family history, and her artistic talent have given us a treasured legacy. Parts of this legacy are shared here for those who enjoy learning or reminiscing about America's family farming history.

Mom was an admirer of Laura Ingalls Wilder's books, which are memories of a pioneer girlhood: Little House In The Big Woods, Little House On The Prairie, On The Banks of Plum Creek and so on. She was introduced to them in teachers' college, and when she grew up she read them to her own children in the evenings. On trips to South Dakota, we would visit homestead sites and historical markers connected to the books. Years later, when Mom and I traveled to South Dakota to bury Dad's ashes, we stopped at the annual Laura Ingalls Wilder Pageant in De Smet, South Dakota, where they put on a play about Wilder's life. Wilder's books inspired Mom to write her own memories.

I think Mom's primary intention for writing The Farm Story was as a document to pass down to new generations within the family. But it was more than that. When I asked her why she took pictures of the farm, she said because it was "a way of life that is disappearing." She was well aware that family farming life was becoming more and more rare—especially the use of horses on farms. Mom was right: the small farm way of life is disappearing. Although this work is a snapshot of my family's particular farm history from 1902 to 1950, her story illustrates the lives of many families residing in rural America during this time of great international change.

Mom believed a full and well-balanced life had to include a hobby, and hers was family history. Nobody else in the immediate family was as interested in this, but she corresponded with relatives and people in other countries who were interested and shared her genealogy hobby. She made friends with scores of distant relatives whom she would visit on trips to research a branch of the family. She would go to historical society meetings—Cincinnati Historical Society and Hamilton County's Historical Society meetings—where she met other like-minded researchers.

Why was my mother so interested in family history? She would always say "These are my ancestors." I think she felt a very personal connection to each person, wanted to know their stories, and wanted their stories preserved. When she'd start telling someone her family history, it was a way of declaring herself and her work: she wouldn't say "our ancestors", she'd say "my ancestors", as if to say, 'This is who I am, and this is where I come from, and this is the work I have done.'

In 1949, my parents moved to Cincinnati where a job awaited Dad after World War II. The job was selling A.B.Dick offset printing presses. My parents were both do-it-yourselfers, and Dad was very mechanically inclined. He had studied engineering. Dad was not raised on a farm but in a very small South Dakota town, Onida. His father ran a hardware store, and was a county road surveyor, among other things. So Dad was intimately familiar with farm life even though he didn't grow up on a farm.

When my brother and I were young, probably eight or ten, our parents gave us a little hand-crank mimeograph machine. We loved it and would do little printing jobs on it. I wish I still had it now! Then at some point, Dad got a used A.B.Dick offset press. With a family of four children to support, Dad and Mom started a cottage printing business. While we were growing up, we had the offset press in our pantry (which we called "the offset room"). In our pantry cupboards, there'd be pots and pans in one cupboard, and in another cupboard there'd be printing ink and rollers and printer supplies and parts. It didn't seem unusual to us! The cottage business became quite the family enterprise—we called it CALHEM Duplicating, using all the family members' first names (Chris, Anne, Linda, Helen, Ed, Mark).

The offset printing press was about the size of an old television, maybe 36" x 30" by about 30" wide—a tabletop press. I think the largest size sheet of paper it would print was 11 x 17. First of all, you needed a negative of each page you were printing. We didn't make the negatives in the house; Dad had that done somewhere else. Each negative was exactly the same size as the finished sheet of paper. You positioned it over a light-sensitive metal sheet called the "plate" with a sheet of glass over them both to keep them pressed together. We had what we called a "plate-maker", that was a gooseneck lamp. You shone the light through the negative onto the plate for about 5 or 6 minutes. Then you took the developer—I remember the smell of it very clearly—and rubbed it on the plate, and the image would appear. At that point, the plate was ready to be fastened to the cylinder of the printing press. We did all this in the pantry "offset room".

Mother had a IBM Selectric typewriter, the kind with one of those balls that could change fonts, and she would do the typesetting. We would get small ongoing printing jobs—flyers, handouts, brochures. For example, I remember we printed handouts for an obstetrician's office, church newsletters and Sunday programs, and things for other local organizations. Many Sunday afternoons we kids spent walking around the dining room table collating newsletters while the football or baseball game played on TV.

The offset printing equipment in the pantry, as it turned out, also came in handy for Mom's interest in family history. She would type up her history research and her correspondence on her electric typewriter, and Dad would print copies in the "offset room" to circulate to the whole family. (Of course, this was all before computers made such tasks so much easier.)

For as long as I can remember, Mom was interested in documenting the history of the family and her memories of growing up on the farm. She started collecting her notes for The Farm Story during the 1960s. I was probably in junior high when she started actually writing it; I remember that by the time I was in high school, she had a little corner in the dining room that was her office. She had the electric typewriter there, and a bookcase full of genealogy notebooks of research she had done.

Dad was genuinely supportive of her interest in family history. When my folks retired, they traveled together to county court houses, libraries and cemeteries across the country in a little camper, researching and documenting their gems of discovery. I remember once when they came to visit me in Chicago, she wanted to follow up on her research and was eager to go to see this cemetery and visit that cemetery. I remember Dad patted her knee and said, "Whatever you want, Mama-san."

The first version of The Farm Story was typed in our dining room, printed in the pantry, published in a limited edition in 1990, and given to the extended family with a few copies of black and white photos included. The photos here are another facet of my parents' collaboration. Mom always said that Dad courted her in the darkroom. Dad's hobby was photography, and when he first left South Dakota to soldier in World War II, he left his camera in Mom's safekeeping. Following her passion, she used it to document the farm she was leaving and that was so much a part of who she grew up to be.

Mom said that her father didn't like women to do fieldwork, but he needed their help at times, so they would do things like drive the tractors. When they did, he would rig up an umbrella on the tractor to shield them from the sun. Nevertheless, Mom's mother Verna seemed to be pretty used to fieldwork. She drove the buck rake, and there are photos of her working in the field and driving horses. Verna started that chicken business, while it also was her job to make sure that all the meals were cooked and served.

Mom studied to be a teacher, like others in the family, and was quite content not to marry a farmer. Still, the farmer's do-it-yourself approach was part of what my parents brought to their new life in the city. On the farm, part of the women's job had been to feed the field hands, and Mom became a great cook. She continued to do a lot of the things she did when she lived on the farm. She still made bread, pie, applesauce, everything. She made the best pie I have ever eaten in my life. We ate a lot of fresh vegetables. We also had more homemade clothes, since Mom was an expert seamstress, another skill she learned growing up on the farm.

We went family camping, starting from when we were very young. Evelyn's family lived next door to us and we all camped together. Our neighbors and friends didn't go camping. Loving to be outdoors and playing in nature was something that I think was part of the farm culture that followed Mom and Evelyn to the city suburbs and was passed down to us kids.

Sometimes our family would go back to the farm to visit. We never stayed on the Ackley farm where Bliss still lived; we stayed at our Aunt Dorothy's, the Sauder farm. I remember both farms as a wonderful world. My South Dakota cousins were about the same age I was, but they were driving tractors at the age of nine, they were riding horses, and they had all this exciting knowledge that we didn't have. We just got a little peek into that world. We got to ride the horses and chase the hogs, ride in hay wagons, drive the tractor—and it was just great. I loved the smell of the barn. We watched Uncle Harold milk the cows and squirt milk at the cats; the cats would sit up and catch it in their mouths. How wonderful! And there was fresh-from-the-cow milk for breakfast.

I went back to the farm with Mom after Bliss died, just before the house was torn down. It was all weathered, and you had to watch out where you stepped or you could fall through the floor. She was saying goodbye to the place. She and I went back again after Dad died, when the house was totally gone and there was nothing except the fallen-down barn and some rusting, antiquated farm equipment to let you know that anybody had ever lived there.

The Ackley farmland is still owned by Ackley family descendants. Dorothy's son Gene owns the south half where the farmstead was and his brother Jerry owns the north half. They grow soybeans and corn. When the farm house was torn down, someone saved the blue glass lightning rod insulating balls that Mom mentions in this book in connection with Evelyn's birth story. Mom kept them, and Dad made stands to display them. Now I have them, and use them for garden ornaments. A small bit of the farm house to remind me of The Farm Story every day.

In March 2000 my Mother and I signed a contract giving me copyright to her manuscript, The Farm Story, including photos and written documents.

I spent many hours collecting, organizing, and adding to her material with taped interviews of her reminiscences.

That little hand crank mimeograph and our family's cottage printing business had turned into my lifetime "hobby" and I co-founded a small publishing company that published five books, all of which I printed myself on a small printing press in my basement.

My vision in 2000 was to publish Mom's manuscript and photos together in a book. Recent advances in on-demand self-publishing have now made this possible, and I only wish she could have held this book in her own hands.

Dad died in 1994 and Mom lived, mostly independently, to 86 years old. A few months before she died, I was able to give her a Certificate of Recognition from Smithsonian Magazine. She was thrilled to learn that her photo of the '49 Ford was a semi-finalist in the first Smithsonian Magazine photo contest. The photo was published in the June 2004 issue, and she proudly showed it to all who visited her in the hospice facility. She died July 5, 2004.

I still have more than 20 of her three-ring binders of family history in my basement—personal letters, family genealogy, some ancestry she traced back to the 1300s, stories she got her grandparents to tell her, stories about her great-grandfather being a teamster on the Erie Canal, and more—all waiting to be digitally formatted or published when I retire.

The apple doesn't fall far …

Thank you for taking the time to read The Farm Story. If you feel like it, drop me a note and share your thoughts or reminiscences.

— Christine Leslie Johnson
thefarmstory.helenjohnson@gmail.com

Crossing the Plains By Automobile

Broad horizon,
  Broad as the eye can see
  And beyond
  The vast blue bowl of the sky
  Turned upside down on the
  Vast brown dish of the prairie.

The emptiness accented by works of man—
  Poles, trees, grain elevators,
  Oil wells bowing and scraping—
  Like prehistoric birds pulling
  Endless worms from the depths.

All of these—
But most of all—
  The vast blue bowl arching over
  The vast brown plate.

— 1996, Evelyn Ackley Christensen (1923-2006)

11459848R00065

Made in the USA
Charleston, SC
26 February 2012